MOTOR RACING
THROUGH
THE FIFTIES

Peter Lewis
Motor Racing Correspondent of "The Observer" 1954-1960

Foreword by Hugh Lewis

Dedication
This book is dedicated to 18 month old twins, Felix and Harvey Lewis, who have yet to see their first motor race.

Book Design & Illustrations by
John Hanson

Published 1992 by
Naval & Military Press,
5 Buckingham Street,
Strand,
London WC2N 6BS

Typeset, Printed and Bound by
Bourne Press Ltd.,
Bournemouth.

ISBN 1 897632 15 0

"They Lived to Race"

MOTOR RACING THROUGH THE FIFTIES

Contents

Juan Manuel Fangio

Juan Manuel Fangio on his way to victory during a scorching heatwave in the 1955 Argentine Grand Prix. Having won the World Championship of Drivers five times between 1951 and 1957, he retired at the age of 47, after the French Grand Prix in July 1958. **(Mercedes-Benz AG)**

MOTOR RACING THROUGH THE FIFTIES

Acknowledgements

It is not easy to get together seventy-four pictures to illustrate words that were written in the fifties. I was able to do so thanks to Geoffrey Goddard, Cyril Posthumus, and Norman Newbatt who produced bulging folders of pictures that brought back vivid memories of the fifties.

Thanks also to Chris Gill, librarian of the National Motor Museum, who made available at very short notice the thousands of pictures housed at Beaulieu, and to Joan Williamson, the ever helpful librarian at the Royal Automobile Club in Pall Mall.

Mercedes-Benz AG in Stuttgart found pictures that nobody else has, and sent them by return of post, whilst LAT Photographic and Quadrant/Autocar Picture Libraries could not have been more helpful. Thanks also to Tony Brooks for sorting through his files and producing some splendid action shots, and to Ann Harris at Jaguar Daimler Heritage Trust. And thanks to my son Hugh Lewis, who has been so much involved at every stage in the design and production of this book.

Last but by no means least my grateful thanks to Cyril Posthumus for encouraging me to go ahead with the book, for reading the proofs and giving his valuable comments, and just for remembering so much about the glorious fifties.

PETER LEWIS
Northwood,
October 1992

Foreword

When I first became interested in motor racing in 1956, my father was Motor Racing correspondent for the Observer newspaper.

I was fortunate enough to accompany him to many of the races described in these pages and it was my job to record the race order lap by lap and note down every incident or retirement. Quite why he went to such lengths to be so comprehensive in his reporting of a race always surprised me. Motor racing then did not enjoy the support and media coverage it does today. A fantastic race like the Italian Grand Prix at Monza in 1953 could well be sub-edited down to a couple of hundred words or less and given no more prominence than the reporting of a minor fourth division football match.

To have read a piece that said little more than that after a closely fought race (Fangio won by just over two seconds from Farina) would have given little impression of the full drama of the events described so vividly in Chapter Two.

My part in all this was largely unpaid, save for the odd half of shandy after the story had been phoned over to the paper. However, it was immensely rewarding. How many other schoolboys got the chance to rub shoulders with 'greats' like Fangio, Moss, Hawthorn and Ascari?

Of course, in the 1950's, getting close to the drivers was not a privilege reserved for the Press. For the price of a paddock pass you could stand within feet of your heroes as their cars were warmed up prior to the race.

There were no exclusive enclosures for drivers, sponsors and their guests. Corporate entertainment was virtually non-existent. Few drivers that I can remember arrived at the circuits in helicopters or private planes. Indeed they often had to rely on far more modest forms of transport.

I can recall an incident when Harry Schell had to borrow a motor-scooter to try to get through the race day traffic queuing for Silverstone. He was late for final practice and the problem was further aggravated by a motor-cycle policeman who halted Schell's rapid progress through the crowds until he could be convinced by those of us in the queue that this was really one of the Grand Prix drivers.

Imagine not recognising Nigel Mansell or Ayrton Senna today!

The sport was very different then. Sponsorship as we know it now did not exist. There were the 'works' teams and the private entrants. The front row of the grid at Silverstone could accommodate four cars, rather than the two it does today. The difference in qualifying times between pole position and the back of the grid was often as much as a half a minute.

Yet the outcome of any race was never as predictable as it sometimes seems to be today. Technology had not reached the point where it could make one marque virtually unbeatable. The 'works' teams had the edge but there was always the chance that Moss, in a privately entered car, would beat them all on sheer driving ability. Fangio was another whose outstanding skill could cancel out the differential between his own and quicker cars.

The great drivers of that era were quite a different breed. Few, with the notable exception of Moss, maintained any sort of fitness regimes. Many, like Mike Hawthorn and Peter Collins were known to enjoy the odd drink, even on the night before race day.

I remember my father being woken in his hotel in Spa by the sound of Hawthorn and Rodney Walkerley of 'The Motor' playing football with a dustbin lid in the courtyard below his room at 2.30 in the morning, with the start of the Belgian Grand Prix only hours away!

Both Hawthorn and Collins were notorious practical jokers. On another occasion in Spa they got wind of the fact that Harry Schell had planned a midnight assignation in his hotel room with an attractive young local lady, who shall remain nameless. They promptly removed the bed from his room and replaced it with the 3-wheel bubble car that Schell used to get to and from the circuit. Schell's comments on discovering this, as he crept into his room, are not recorded.

Off the circuit there was a great deal of fun and camaraderie amongst the drivers. On the circuits they gave me and thousands who watched them tremendous pleasure and entertainment.

The decade this book covers is also important for the superb Grand Prix cars it produced; like the beautiful 250F Maserati and the fast but fragile Lancia-Ferraris. It saw the return to Grand Prix racing of Mercedes-Benz in 1954 and the first serious British challenge to Italian domination, in the distinctive shape of the Vanwalls in 1957. The success of the rear-engined Cooper-Climax in 1958 and 1959 set the pattern for all the future Grand Prix car design.

But above all, this book is about the men who raced these cars. They lived to race and they loved to race and they did so with a spirit of competitiveness and sporting rivalry that will probably never be seen again on the world's Grand Prix circuits.

Re-reading our notes more than 30 years on, I'm glad we kept such comprehensive records.

HUGH LEWIS
October 1992

Chapter 1

FRENCH GRAND PRIX
5 JULY 1953

The Circuit

RHEIMS

60 Laps of 8.300 KM

498 KM = 309.44 MILES

The French Grand Prix which was run at Rouen in 1952 returned to the much faster Rheims circuit for 1953. It is a road circuit, roughly triangular in shape, and set in the attractive open countryside six miles to the west of Rheims. The northern flank of the circuit is part of the main road to Soissons, and the circuit was extended for the 1953 race to include a new corner (Virage de Muizon) which in effect lengthened the section of the Soissons road leading to Thillois.

From the main grandstand it is possible—with a pair of binoculars—to see nearly two thirds of the circuit and in particular the Soissons road where the cars break out of a wooded area and streak down to Thillois hairpin which is in fact a very slow corner. Straightening up and accelerating out of the corner without losing a foot of road can mean the difference between victory and defeat on the last lap of a close-fought race. Mike Hawthorn proved the point when he won the French Grand Prix in 1953.

The difficult and dangerous flat-out bend under the Dunlop bridge is soon after the start.

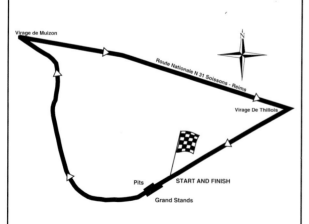

Starting Grid

L. VILLORESI	F. BONETTO	A. ASCARI
FERRARI	MASERATI	FERRARI
2.41.9	2.41.5	2.41.2

J. F. GONZALEZ	J. M. FANGIO
MASERATI	MASERATI
2.42.4	2.42.0

O. MARIMON	J. M. HAWTHORN	G. FARINA
MASERATI	FERRARI	FERRARI
2.44.7	2.43.5	2.42.5

L. ROSIER	E. DE GRAFFENRIED
FERRARI	MASERATI
2.49.6	2.46.1

S. MOSS	F. R. GERARD	B. BIRA
COOPER-ALTA	COOPER-BRISTOL	CONNAUGHT
2.55.7	2.54.2	2.53.2

E. BAYOL	K. WHARTON
OSCA	COOPER-BRISTOL
2.56.9	2.55.8

Y. G-CABANTOUS	P. COLLINS	L. MACKLIN
H.W.M.	H.W.M.	H.W.M.
3.06.7	3.02.0	2.57.2

H. SCHELL	R. SALVADORI
GORDINI	CONNAUGHT
3.25.8	3.23.0

M. TRINTIGNANT	J. BEHRA	J. CLAES
GORDINI	GORDINI	CONNAUGHT
No practice time	No practice time	4.06.5

L. CHIRON	R. MIERES
OSCA	GORDINI
No practice time	No practice time

The Race of the Century

*T*he bar of the Hotel Welcome in Rheims was thick with tobacco smoke and noisy with the chatter of motor-racing enthusiasts, journalists, mechanics, representatives of the tyre and fuel companies—and the inevitable hangers-on, for sooner or later most of the motor-racing crowd find their way to the friendly atmosphere of the Hotel Welcome. The topic of conversation was a fair-haired Englishman, only twenty-four years old, who in practice for the French Grand Prix of 1953 had streaked round the Rheims road circuit—in the rolling open countryside some six miles to the west of the town—at an average speed of nearly 115 m.p.h. His name was John Michael Hawthorn, in his first season with the fabulous Ferrari team and still very much a new boy—still learning, in fact, from his team-mates, the maestro Ascari and his countrymen Villoresi and Farina.

Hawthorn was, without a doubt, the fastest of the British drivers entered for the race; but in fairness to the others—including Stirling Moss and Peter Collins—it must be emphasised that they were driving British cars. And in 1953 there was no combination of British car and driver that stood the remotest chance of winning a world championship event against the Italian Ferraris and Maseratis. But Hawthorn in a Ferrari was a very different proposition, and there were several people in the Welcome that night who would have gladly backed him for a place had there been any bookmakers present.

On the Sunday, as a twelve-hour sports-car race drew to a close, the tired spectators who had watched the race since midnight were joined by others who had come to see the continuation of a season-long duel between the two Italian teams of Ferrari and Maserati, and the continuation of a duel for the World Championship of 1953 between the Argentine ace, Juan Fangio, champion in 1951, and the Italian ace, Alberto Ascari, champion in 1952.

Soon after the sports-car race had ended in a fine victory for the Jaguar driven by Stirling Moss and Peter Whitehead, the Grand Prix cars were wheeled on to the circuit. This was Hawthorn's fourth world championship event with the Ferrari team, and as he walked along the front of the pits to where the Ferraris were lined up he set a thousand tongues wagging.

Who was the fair-haired, six-foot youngster with the bow-tie who towered head and shoulders over most of the other drivers? Was he really good enough to race in the crack Ferrari team? Well they might have asked, for it was only fifteen months previously, at the Goodwood Easter Meeting, that Mike Hawthorn had driven a single-seater racing car for the first time.

At the Sussex circuit, in a brand-new, unpainted 2-litre Cooper-Bristol tuned by his father and only delivered a few days before the meeting, Hawthorn won two races and finished second to the $4\frac{1}{2}$-litre Ferrari Thinwall Special driven by Gonzalez in the big race. From that day onwards the boyish-looking driver—every inch an Englishman both on and off the track—climbed the ladder of success two steps at a time. In race report after race report there were references to 'Hawthorn and that astonishing Cooper-Bristol'.

In race after race, his bulky form wedged in the cockpit of the Cooper-Bristol, he fought a lone battle against the powerful factory teams. In the Belgian Grand Prix of 1952, his first race on the Continent, he was fourth, behind two Ferraris and a Gordini—miles ahead of any other British car. In the British Grand Prix at Silverstone he finished third, behind the Ferraris of Ascari and Taruffi; whilst in the Dutch Grand Prix he brought the Cooper-Bristol home fourth, behind the Ferraris of Ascari, Farina and Villoresi.

Enzo Ferrari was not slow to act. If the boy was good enough to race against the Italian aces in a car that stood little chance of beating them, why not give him an Italian car to drive? And so Mike Hawthorn signed with Ferrari for 1953—the first Englishman to join a foreign team since 1937, when Richard Seaman signed with Mercedes-Benz.

On that Sunday afternoon in July at Rheims, as the cars were positioned on the starting grid under a clear blue sky and in the shimmering heat of a summer's day, Mike Hawthorn was about to make a tremendous, unforgettable impact on the motor-racing world in one of the most exciting races ever run.

Ascari held pole position (nearest to the starter) on the front row of the grid, having put up fastest time in practice. Next to the Ferrari was the Maserati of Bonetto, then the Ferrari of Villoresi. On the second row were two cars only, the Maseratis of Fangio and Gonzalez; and on the third row three cars again—the Ferraris of Farina and Hawthorn together with the Maserati of Marimon.

From the moment the starter dropped his flag the French Grand Prix had all the makings of a great race. From the second row Gonzalez made a fantastic start, his fuel

Crouched low in the cockpit of his Maserati, Gonzalez leads Fangio's Maserati at the start of the 1953 French G.P. Gonzalez started with a half-full tank and rocketed through from the second row of the grid.
(Geoffrey Goddard)

When Mike Hawthorn won the 1953 French G.P. he became the first Englishman to win the French classic since Sir Henry Segrave at Tours in 1923. Segrave drove the 2-litre Sunbeam No. 2 for 496 miles at an average of 75.30 mph.
(National Motor Museum)

When Hawthorn (Cooper-Bristol)
won the Lavant Cup at Goodwood
in April 1952 it was his first 'drive'
in a single-seater and was followed
by good placings in the Belgian,
British and Dutch classics. Ferrari
signed Hawthorn for 1953.

From the Dunlop Bridge a
priviledged group watches
Hawthorn closing on the Ferraris
of Farina and Villoresi before
breaking away from his team-
mates and challenging Fangio.
(Geoffrey Goddard)

Hawthorn grins across at Fangio
(No. 18) as the Ferrari and
Maserati race side by side in a
fierce duel that lasted for over half
the race. Ten times they were side
by side at 150 mph.
(Quadrant/Autocar)

tanks only half full; and as the cars swept past the grandstand and along the line of crowded pit counters he went into the lead, crouched over the wheel in the characteristic style that had earned him the title of 'The Prairie Bull'.

As Gonzalez sliced through between his team mates Fangio and Bonetto and pulled away rapidly, the Ferrari drivers were immediately faced with the problem of whether to risk blowing up their engines by trying to keep up with the Maserati. Gonzalez would have to stop for fuel sooner or later, but when he did so it was imperative that he had not built up such a commanding lead that he could take on fuel and still retain first place.

Gonzalez had a problem as well, for he knew how much fuel would be required and approximately how long the fuel stop would take. He needed not five, ten, or fifteen seconds but at least twenty seconds.

The Rheims circuit has a very fast back leg, a two-mile section of the main road from Rheims to Soissons, and by looking across country from the grandstands one can see the cars break cover as they leave a wooded area and sweep downhill at 150 m.p.h. to Thillois Corner and the straight that leads back to the pits.

On this memorable Sunday, as the tail end of the field swept under the Dunlop bridge at the end of the pits area, and to the right and out of view, Gonzalez was already lining himself up for Muizon corner and the Soissons road. The seconds ticked by and then suddenly the field burst into view. In a tight bunch the Maseratis and Ferraris tore down the back leg to Thillois corner, one car fractionally ahead of the rest. Then Gonzalez was through the corner and accelerating up the straight, the pack hard on his heels.

As the red cars of Italy tore through the pit area at 150 m.p.h., exhaust notes crisp and urgent for the chase had just started, it was Gonzalez, Ascari, Villoresi, Fangio, Hawthorn, Bonetto, Marimon and Farina. All red cars—four Maseratis and four Ferraris.

Slowly but surely Gonzalez consolidated his lead. On the second lap he was four seconds ahead, lapping at over 112 m.p.h. Two laps later he had built up his lead to five and a half seconds. Behind Gonzalez three Ferrari drivers—Villoresi, Ascari and Hawthorn—were locked in a tremendous struggle for second place, slightly ahead of Fangio and Farina. The Ferraris were so close together that every time they passed the pits only half a second separated the nose of the first from the tail of the third one. It was a three-decker sandwich, with the filling continually changing as first Ascari, then Villoresi, then Hawthorn took the lead.

With ten laps completed, Gonzalez had built up a lead of seven seconds. He was coaxing every ounce of power out of the Maserati, knowing only too well that at half distance he would have to stop for fuel. With twenty laps completed—one third of the race distance—Gonzalez led by twenty seconds from the Ferraris and was averaging

113.3 m.p.h. A lap later Fangio was in amongst the Ferraris, ready to challenge for the lead when his team mate Gonzalez stopped to refuel.

It was on the twenty-ninth lap that Gonzalez made his move. As the Maserati accelerated out of Thillois, twenty seconds ahead of the Ferraris and Fangio's Maserati, the churns of fuel were ready in the pit. As Gonzalez braked to a halt, a score of stopwatches in the Press Stand started to tick away the seconds. Five...ten...fifteen. If Gonzalez did not get away soon he would lose the lead, for the Ferraris were through Thillois.

Another five seconds passed—and then, in a crescendo of noise, Gonzalez dropped from first place to sixth as five cars tore through the pits area led by Hawthorn, Ascari and Fangio. Gonzalez was far from beaten. A few seconds later, having refuelled in twenty-seven seconds, the Maserati accelerated away from the pits, Gonzalez crouched low in the cockpit, determined to whittle down those precious seconds and to challenge for the lead once more.

Out in front, Fangio was in first place, Hawthorn well up and not giving away an inch, Ascari just behind and marvelling at the way this comparatively new boy was mixing it with Fangio. Surely the Englishman was not going to be able to keep up this blistering pace for another 150 miles. Then, to the astonishment of Ascari, who could do nothing to prevent it, the Maserati and Ferrari started to draw away, Hawthorn and Fangio battling wheel to wheel as though they had only another half a dozen laps to complete instead of another twenty-eight. This was real motor-racing of a kind rarely seen, and the other drivers in this French Grand Prix of 1953 sat back and watched the drama.

For lap after lap Hawthorn and Fangio kept close company, never more than a car's length apart, frequently racing abreast. The crowd in the grandstand, in the pits, down at Thillois Hairpin and lining the finishing straight, went wild with excitement. Roughly every two and three-quarter minutes the two cars tore through the pits area, and on ten separate occasions they were side by side at 150 m.p.h., so close that Hawthorn was able to read the engine revolution counter in Fangio's Maserati as he grinned across at the Argentine driver.

Fangio tried every trick of the trade to shake off the young Englishman, but this was Hawthorn's day and no one was going to stop him winning his first World Championship event. And no one was going to stop the astonishing Gonzalez from getting to the front again. Driving like the wind, and on top of his form, he passed Farina; then he took Ascari for third place. His magnificent effort, as lap by lap he recovered the vital seconds lost during the refuelling stop, went almost unnoticed as the battle raged between Fangio and Hawthorn. But suddenly Gonzalez was in third place and a somewhat surprised Ascari lay fourth.

There were several incidents that will long be remembered by those of us in the Press

Box who were fortunate enough to witness Hawthorn's triumph that day. On one occasion, as the two cars streaked through the pits area, a slower driver was in the way on the approach to the right-hand curve beyond the pits. Hawthorn held a slender lead, not more than a few feet, and had he kept to his line Fangio would have had to drop back behind the slower car, thus allowing Hawthorn to forge ahead. As the Maserati and Ferrari closed like an express train on the slower driver, Hawthorn pulled over and put his wheels on the grass beside the track so that he and Fangio could pass together. The crowd roared its approval of such sportsmanship, and Fangio raised his gloved hand in salute.

On another part of the course, at Muizon Corner, Hawthorn went into the corner so close to the Maserati that he bumped its tail. As the two cars accelerated, Hawthorn signalled his apology but Fangio just grinned back. He said afterwards that he thought Hawthorn had bumped him on purpose, wanting to get by and unable to do so because Fangio was slower and in the way. Some drivers would have objected most strongly to being bumped, especially if they thought this was the reason, but Fangio's grin and acceptance of Hawthorn's apology was typical of the sportsmanship shown by these two fine drivers on that memorable Sunday afternoon.

From where he sat in the cockpit of his Maserati, Gonzalez had a grandstand view of the dramatic closing seconds of a 100 m.p.h. plus duel that had lasted nearly one and a half hours. He saw as neat a piece of tactical driving as he had ever seen.

For several laps, as Fangio had led Hawthorn past the pits, the Ferrari being towed along in the slipstream of the Maserati, Hawthorn had pulled out of the slipstream, passed Fangio and then dropped back again. He was, in fact, rehearsing his final spurt for the last lap.

On the final lap, as Fangio and Hawthorn streaked down Route Nationale 31 (the Soissons road) to Thillois Corner for the last time, Fangio led Hawthorn by a car's length, and Gonzalez was closing on them both. Fangio and Hawthorn braked for Thillois and went into the corner almost as one; and as Fangio held a slide coming out of the corner, Hawthorn was already straightened up and accelerating. This was the final spurt that he had rehearsed, and as the Ferrari streaked towards the chequered flag Hawthorn inexorably opened up the longest gap between his Ferrari and Fangio's Maserati in 150 miles of duelling.

Hawthorn crossed the line no more than seven lengths—or one second—ahead of Fangio, and the welcoming roar of applause swelled to a crescendo as Gonzalez closed right up on Fangio and crossed the line with his front wheels level with Fangio's rear ones. Three seconds later, Ascari finished the race in fourth place.

After 309 miles of racing at an average speed of 113.65 m.p.h. only 4.6 seconds spanned the first four cars. No wonder journalists described it as the race of the century, and no wonder the Ferrari mechanics mobbed Mike Hawthorn as he stood up in the cockpit, for the young Englishman with the bow-tie had maintained Ferrari's unbroken sequence of world championship victories and in doing so had beaten one of the greatest racing drivers of all time in a straight fight.

That night, in the bar of the Hotel Welcome, they drank Mike Hawthorn's health again and again, and dawn had already broken when at last the bar was empty. The toast was to the first Englishman to win a *Grand Epreuve* since Richard Seaman won the 1938 German Grand Prix for Mercedes-Benz, and the first Englishman to win the French Grand Prix since Sir Henry Segrave had been victorious with a 2- litre Sunbeam at Tours thirty years previously.

And there was another toast as well—to that ebullient, dynamic character from Argentina, Froilan Gonzalez, who on that day had also given a fantastic performance.

Results
60 Laps

1.	J.M. HAWTHORN	FERRARI	2 HR 44 MIN 18.6 SEC
			182.888 KPH (113.641 MPH)
2.	J.M. FANGIO	MASERATI	2 HR 44 MIN 19.6 SEC
3.	J.F. GONZALEZ	MASERATI	2 HR 44 MIN 20.0 SEC
4.	A. ASCARI	FERRARI	2 HR 44 MIN 23.2 SEC
5.	G. FARINA	FERRARI	2 HR 45 MIN 26.2 SEC
6.	L. VILLORESI	FERRARI	2 HR 45 MIN 34.5 SEC
7.	E. DE GRAFFENRIED	MASERATI	58 LAPS
8.	L. ROSIER	FERRARI	56 LAPS
9.	O. MARIMON	MASERATI	55 LAPS
10.	J. BEHRA	GORDINI	55 LAPS
11.	F.R. GERARD	COOPER-BRISTOL	55 LAPS
12.	J. CLAES	CONNAUGHT	53 LAPS
13.	P. COLLINS	H.W.M.	52 LAPS
14.	Y. GIRAUD-CABANTOUS	H.W.M.	50 LAPS

FASTEST LAP: **J.M. FANGIO** ON LAP 25 AND **A. ASCARI** ON LAP 37
2 MIN 41.1 SEC AT **186.539 KPH (115.909 MPH)**.

Retirements

R. SALVADORI	CONNAUGHT	LAP 2 - Ignition
H. SCHELL	GORDINI	LAP 4 - Engine
R. MIERES	GORDINI	LAP 4 - Rear axle
L. MACKLIN	H.W.M.	LAP 9 - Clutch
M. TRINTIGNANT	GORDINI	LAP 14 - Transmission
K. WHARTON	COOPER-BRISTOL	LAP 17 - Engine
E. BAYOL	OSCA	LAP 18
B. BIRA	CONNAUGHT	LAP 29 - Transmission
S. MOSS	COOPER-ALTA	LAP 38 - Clutch
F. BONETTO	MASERATI	LAP 42 - Engine
L. CHIRON	OSCA	LAP 43

Chapter 2

ITALIAN GRAND PRIX
13 SEPTEMBER 1953

The Circuit

MONZA

80 laps of 6.3 KM

504.0 KM = 313.17 MILES

Twelve-and-a-half miles north of Milan, in what used to be the Royal Park, the Monza circuit is set in a vast expanse of parkland—criss-crossed by roads—and has been the home of the Italian Grand Prix for most years since it was first run in 1921 at Brescia.

It is a road circuit—roughly L shaped—where spectators in the vast grandstand have a superb view of the start line and pits, also the straight leading to the Curva Grande. The circuit is one of the fastest in the championship series and lends itself to the kind of high-speed cutting and thrusting at close quarters that delights the thousands of Italians who make the annual pilgrimage to Monza for the Italian Grand Prix. For it is *the* race of the year for them.

After some sensational duelling for lap after lap in the 1953 race, which culminated in a multiple accident at Curva di Vedano just before the pits, Fangio crossed the line first in his Maserati. His average speed was 110.685 mph and he had put up fastest lap as well at 113.194 mph.

Starting Grid

G. FARINA FERRARI 2.03.9	**J. M. FANGIO** MASERATI 2.03.2	**A. ASCARI** FERRARI 2.02.7
J. M. HAWTHORN FERRARI 2.04.9	**L. VILLORESI** FERRARI 2.04.6	**O. MARIMON** MASERATI 2.04.1
E. de GRAFFENRIED MASERATI 2.05.9	**M. TRINTIGNANT** GORDINI 2.05.7	**F. BONETTO** MASERATI 2.05.1
S. MANTOVANI MASERATI 2.07.5	**U. MAGLIOLI** FERRARI 2.06.9	**S. MOSS** COOPER-ALTA 2.06.6
H. SCHELL GORDINI 2.08.0	**R. SALVADORI** CONNAUGHT 2.08.0	**E. BAYOL** OSCA 2.07.8
K. McALPINE CONNAUGHT 2.09.5	**L. ROSIER** FERRARI 2.09.3	**R. MIERES** GORDINI 2.08.7
C. LANDI MASERATI 2.12.8	**P. CARINI** FERRARI 2.11.2	**K. WHARTON** COOPER-BRISTOL 2.10.1
A. BROWN COOPER-BRISTOL 2.14.8	**B. BIRA** MASERATI 2.13.6	**J. FAIRMAN** CONNAUGHT 2.13.5
L. MACKLIN H.W.M. 2.18.2	**J. FITCH** H.W.M. 2.18.1	**L. CHIRON** OSCA 2.15.0
J. CLAES CONNAUGHT 2.28.2	**H. STUCK** A.F.M.-BRISTOL 2.24.1	**Y. G-CABANTOUS** H.W.M. 2.20.8

Curva di Lesmo

Curva Grande

START AND FINISH

Curva de Vedano

Pits and Grandstands

Fangio

Four-Car Duel at Monza

The Monza Autodrome, an artificial road circuit in what was once the Royal Park of Monza, twelve and a half miles from Milan, has been the scene of many a fierce battle between rival teams. Time and time again the Italian Grand Prix on this ultra-fast circuit has not only written finis to the season but has added another breathtaking chapter to the history of motor-racing. Such a chapter was written on September 13th, 1953 but few if any of the thousands who journeyed to the Autodrome—by train, tram, bus, private car or bicycle—on that memorable Sunday could have imagined in their wildest dreams the fantastic battle that was to take place that afternoon between the rival teams of Ferrari and Maserati.

The Italians expected a battle of some sort, for to them the Italian Grand Prix is *the* race of the year and Italian drivers know full well that the crowds will be disappointed if they do not see cut-and-thrust motor-racing of the highest order. But the Italian Grand Prix of 1953 was not just an exciting race—it was a fabulous one.

The pace was fast and furious even during the practice sessions, and the fastest driver on the first day of official practice was Alberto Ascari, the 1952 world champion and No. 1 Ferrari driver, who streaked round the 3.9-mile circuit in 2 min. 2.9 sec., an average speed of over 113 m.p.h. Juan Fangio, the 1951 world champion and No. 1 Maserati driver, could not equal Ascari's time although he did get down to 2 min. 3.2 sec. on the second and final day of practice. However, Ascari capped this with a time of 2 min. 2.7 sec., and if Fangio wanted the best position on the starting grid he had to save another second somewhere. He might have done so during the closing minutes of the practice session if he had not lost a rear tyre at 120 m.p.h. The Argentine driver controlled the Maserati superbly and pulled over to the side of the track without damage to his car or to himself. He was, however, a very shaken man and understandably so.

That night, as the Maseratis and Ferraris were given a final pre-race check, the question was posed time and time again: Ferrari or Maserati, Ascari or Fangio? And as is always the case with the fiercely partisan Italians the arguments were long and often heated.

For two seasons, following the introduction of Formula 2 (a maximum engine capacity of 2 litres unsupercharged), the 'Prancing Horse' insignia of Ferrari had dominated the scene. In 1952 Ferrari had won every single world championship event, and it was not until the end of the season that Maserati entered the fray. They did so at Monza in the Italian Grand Prix when the Formula 2 Maserati made its début in the hands of Gonzalez and Bonetto. Ascari led Gonzalez over the line by just over a minute, setting the pattern for the 1953 season. Once again Ferrari were to be the victors, but this was no walk-over like 1952, for the Maseratis of Fangio and Gonzalez were a constant threat and every race was closely fought.

The Maseratis were fractionally faster than the Ferraris, but the 'Prancing Horse' cars had superior road holding, and it was only on the really fast circuits such as Spa, Rheims and Monza that the odds were slightly in favour of Maserati.

Mike Hawthorn's superb drive at Rheims gave victory to Ferrari, and at Spa the friendly rivalry in the Maserati camp between Fangio and Gonzalez gave the race to Ferrari. Both drivers tore away from the remainder of the field at the start and had a tremendous scrap between themselves which put both the Maseratis out of the running with little more than a third of the race run.

The odds between Ferrari and Maserati were just about even at Monza, particularly when it was learned that Gonzalez would not be fit to race. Maserati would obviously make an all-out bid to win the last championship event of the year and the last Formula 2 Grand Prix before the introduction of the new formula in 1954. And Fangio, without Gonzalez in his rear view mirror, would obviously be able to give his undivided attention to battling with the Ferraris, and Ascari in particular. He could not wrest the world championship from Ascari, for the brilliant Italian had already collected an unassailable total of points, but he could defeat the Ferraris and thus gain inestimable prestige for Maserati. Make no mistake—the Italian Grand Prix is *the* race of the year so far as the Italians are concerned.

This then was the picture as the red cars of Italy, the blue Gordinis of France, and a handful of cars in British racing green, including Stirling Moss's very rapid, fuel-injected Cooper-Alta which was running on nitromethane, were positioned on the starting grid. The electric atmosphere at Monza as the voluble but knowledgeable Italians pack the vast grandstand opposite the pits, and the public enclosures, is one which once experienced is never forgotten. Few people have summed up the start of a Monza Grand Prix better than an American journalist who visited the Autodrome for the first

The quartet sweeps out of the Curva di Vedano and up towards the pits with the Ferraris of Farina and Ascari narrowly leading from the Maseratis of Marimon and—on the extreme right—Fangio. On the last lap of the race Curva di Vedano was the scene of a spectacular crash.
(Quadrant/Autocar)

In the last championship race of 1953 the battle between Fangio and Marimon in Maseratis and Ascari and Farina in Ferraris was breathtaking. Out in the parkland Farina (No. 6) and Fangio (No. 50) are neck and neck—unruffled, determined and neither giving an inch.
(Cyril Posthumus)

Lap after lap the Ferraris and Maseratis fought for the lead—a lead that was constantly changing. Here, Fangio leads Farina whilst behind them Marimon has closed right up on Ascari.
(Cyril Posthumus)

▲

Fangio leads a three-decker sandwich with Farina (No. 6) on his tail and Marimon on Farina's tail. For nearly three hours there was never more than two seconds between whichever two cars were leading at the time.

(Quadrant/Autocar)

◄

After an unusually bad start, from the front row of the grid, a grimly determined Fangio pulled out all the stops and was lying fourth at the end of the first lap. Only three seconds covered the first four cars.

(Cyril Posthumus)

time in 1953 and said to me 'With these people and this tension it is only a matter of time before someone lights the blue touch paper.' How right he was.

Down on the starting grid some drivers stood by their cars whilst others were already sitting in the cockpit. Ascari, world champion in 1952 and with the championship in the bag for 1953 as well, held pole position—nearest to the starter. The Italian ace was grimly determined to maintain the unbeaten Ferrari record over two seasons. Fangio's Maserati was lined up next to Ascari's car and there was no doubt that the 1951 world champion was equally determined to break the Ferrari sequence. Fangio was sandwiched between two Ferraris, for the third position on the front row was occupied by Farina, world champion in 1950. Farina had been playing second fiddle to Ascari for most of 1953, but there was no reason why he should not make an all-out bid for victory in this last race of the season. The championship had already been decided and Farina was just as free as any driver in any team to 'have a go'.

Behind Ascari, Fangio and Farina—champions all—were twenty-seven other drivers, positioned in order of their practice times, including the young Argentine driver, Onofre Marimon, a protégé of Fangio; the veteran Ferrari driver, Villoresi; fair-haired Mike Hawthorn, victor of the French Grand Prix, Bonetto and Stirling Moss. Although Moss had a very rapid motor car—the Cooper-Alta—it stood very little chance against the Ferraris and Maseratis.

After the flags of the competing nations had been paraded by bearers, the starting grid was cleared of all but a few officials and mechanics. The pit counters were crowded, as was the terrace with its sun parasols above the pits, whilst the grandstands and enclosures were packed solid. The stage was set.

First one engine then another burst into life until the powerful note of each engine was merged into one, the entire grid seemingly straining at the leash and waiting for the flag to drop. The engine note rose to a crescendo as the seconds slipped away and the cars at the back of the grid started to edge forward. Then they were off—closely packed, jockeying for position, every driver thankful that at last the tension was ended.

Momentarily Fangio pushed the nose of his Maserati out in front, but missed a gear change and paid dearly for his error as Ascari, Farina and Marimon rocketed into the lead. Away they went down the straight towards the Curva Grande, a fast right-hand curve that took them out of sight. The seconds ticked by and soon the leaders had turned right and right again at Lesmo, and were tearing down the back leg of the course. Two shallow left-hand curves brought them into sight—streaking down the straight on the far side of the pits.

From the grandstand the cars could be seen but only as flashes of colour between gaps in the hedge lining the straight. Suddenly Marimon's Maserati, in the blue and yellow colours of Argentina, was propelled into the lead like a stone from a catapult, but Ascari quickly answered the challenge and when the cars passed the pits for the first time—having turned right and right again at Vedano Curve—it was Ascari's Ferrari that howled by in the lead. Marimon was almost riding the tail of the Ferrari with Farina, Fangio, and Moss well up. Moss, with the Cooper-Alta, was going like the wind, having been faster on the straights in practice than the 'works' Ferraris! However, a pit stop after only two laps to deal with a suspected oil leak—which was in fact excess oil blowing out of the breather—dropped the Cooper-Alta well back.

Meanwhile, the high-speed foursome of Ascari, Marimon, Fangio and Farina tore round the Autodrome with the regularity of an express train. Two Ferraris and two Maseratis with never more than two or three seconds separating the nose of the leading car and the tail of the fourth car. At intervals of just over two minutes the four red cars tore past the pits. Were they going to be able to keep up this fantastic engine-breaking pace for eighty laps—313 miles—in the oppressive heat of the afternoon? The voluble but knowledgeable Italians loved every minute of it for this was motor-racing at Monza with the gloves off—as it should be.

The Maseratis were faster than the Ferraris but this advantage was outweighed by the superior road-holding qualities of the Ferraris and it was virtually stalemate. Five, eight, ten laps were marked off by the lap scorers and still the high-speed foursome tore round Monza like a train of toy trucks being pulled along on the end of a string.

After ten laps had been completed, Farina led Ascari, Fangio and Marimon, whilst Villoresi had moved his Ferrari into fifth place, and Hawthorn was pushing his Ferrari to the limit, trying to break away from Trintignant's Gordini. So there were two battles going on at the same time and the race average was already 110.5 m.p.h. No wonder tension was mounting in the grandstands. No wonder several fights broke out between rival supporters. After all, this was the final race of the season. What matter if the drivers blew up their cars? What matter if they all got a little excited? 'SIT DOWN...SIT DOWN. Here they come again!'

After twenty laps the picture was unaltered and still the lead chopped and changed as first a Ferrari then a Maserati led the crocodile. On the twenty-ninth lap the crowds in the grandstand rose to their feet as one when all four cars tore across the timing strip dead level as though a white tape had been suspended above the windshields to keep the cars in position.

At half distance—with eighty-five minutes and forty laps completed—there were as many people watching the race as in the opening laps. No one bothered about anything else except the duel for first place being waged as though it were a sprint instead of a full-length Grand Prix. As the leaders streaked past the grandstand towards Curva Grande on the forty-first lap Ascari led Fangio by three-tenths of a second, Fangio led Marimon by three-tenths of a second and Marimon led Farina by three-tenths of a second. Villoresi, in fifth place, was one minute twenty-one seconds behind the leader, still holding Trintignant and Hawthorn at bay.

Then fate took a hand. Marimon, who had more than justified Fangio's faith in him that day, ran off the road and damaged his Maserati. The pit stop that followed, whilst Marimon endeavoured not to show mounting impatience as the car was checked, took six minutes. As he waited, fuming inwardly, the three leaders tore past the pits twice, Fangio snatching a quick, sympathetic look on each occasion.

When at last Marimon eased himself into the cockpit and accelerated away he had dropped back to thirteenth place. He had no chance of winning or even of getting a place in the first three, but he was to play a major part in deciding the victor and the vanquished.

With twenty laps still to go, the three leaders—Ascari, Fangio and Farina—caught up and lapped Villoresi and Hawthorn. It was now a five-decker sandwich and suddenly Marimon was back in the thick of it again—three laps behind the leaders, but obviously intent upon giving what support he could to Fangio, his team leader. This was ridiculous. Four cars on a string had been exciting enough, but six was almost too much for any spectator with a weak heart. And then there were five as Hawthorn dropped back and stayed there to watch and wait. Mike was no fool and this was a very private scrap in which he had no part.

With ten laps to go, it was Ascari, Fangio, Farina—Ferrari, Maserati, Ferrari—and a lap later Farina had somehow pushed Fangio back into third place. But Marimon was there, waiting for an opportunity to help his tutor, and there was nothing that anyone could do to keep his blue and yellow Maserati out of the picture.

With two laps to go, Ascari, Fangio and Farina dead-heated across the timing strip, and next time round only three-quarters of a second separated them. Any one of these three could be the winner after seventy-nine laps of racing in each other's pockets. Who would it be?

The answer came two minutes later, just after the watchers in the grandstand saw Marimon's Maserati, still some laps in arrears, closing on the three leaders down the back leg. The seconds ticked by as the four cars disappeared from view, and in Vedano Curve—which cannot be seen from the grandstand—a last-lap, last-corner drama was played out in a few seconds—seconds that cost Ascari and Ferrari the race.

It was the Italian ace who went into Vedano first in spite of Marimon's last-minute bid and it was the Italian who made an error of judgment. Ascari knew that he would have to leave the corner very fast, in one desperate final burst of speed, in order to hold off Farina and Fangio. But the reigning world champion was not his usual immaculate self that day—understandably so for both Fangio and Farina had made his life a misery for nearly three hours—and in pressing his car to the limit, he spun. Farina, only inches away, swerved to avoid Ascari and braked hard. The wily Fangio grasped this heaven-sent opportunity with both hands and slammed through what little gap there was into the lead just as Marimon, unable to find a way through as Fangio had done, rammed the tail of Ascari's Ferrari so hard that the nose of the Maserati was compressed two feet as though a giant hand had forced it inwards.

And so Juan Manuel Fangio took the chequered flag and led Farina's Ferrari across the line by one and a half seconds, whilst Ascari and Marimon started to walk dejectedly towards the pits. What a race! What a victory for Fangio and what a triumph for Maserati who after being defeated by Ferrari in eight successive world championship races during 1952 (one) and 1953 (seven) snatched a ninth from under the very nose of Alberto Ascari.

Results
80 Laps

1.	J.M. FANGIO	MASERATI	2 HR 49 MIN 45.9 SEC
			178.130 KPH (110.685 MPH)
2.	G. FARINA	FERRARI	2 HR 49 MIN 47.3 SEC
3.	L. VILLORESI	FERRARI	79 LAPS
4.	J.M. HAWTHORN	FERRARI	79 LAPS
5.	M. TRINTIGNANT	GORDINI	79 LAPS
6.	R. MIERES	GORDINI	77 LAPS
7.	S. MANTOVANI/L. MUSSO	MASERATI	76 LAPS
8.	U. MAGLIOLI	FERRARI	76 LAPS
9.	H. SCHELL	GORDINI	75 LAPS
10.	L. CHIRON	OSCA	72 LAPS
11.	B. BIRA	MASERATI	72 LAPS
12.	A. BROWN	COOPER-BRISTOL	70 LAPS
13.	S. MOSS	COOPER-ALTA	70 LAPS
14.	H. STUCK	A.F.M.-BRISTOL	67 LAPS
15.	Y. GIRAUD-CABANTOUS	H.W.M.	67 LAPS
16.	L. ROSIER	FERRARI	65 LAPS

STILL RUNNING WHEN RACE ENDED:

J. FAIRMAN	CONNAUGHT	61 LAPS
K. WHARTON	COOPER-BRISTOL	57 LAPS
K. McALPINE	CONNAUGHT	56 LAPS

FASTEST LAP: J.M. FANGIO (MASERATI) ON LAP 39
2 MIN 4.5 SEC AT 182.168 KPH (113.194 MPH)

Retirements

L. MACKLIN	H.W.M.	LAP 6 - Engine
J. CLAES	CONNAUGHT	LAP 8 - Fuel pipe
J. FITCH	H.W.M.	LAP 15 - Engine
E. BAYOL	OSCA	LAP 18 - Mechanical
C. LANDI	MASERATI	LAP 19 - Piston
R. SALVADORI	CONNAUGHT	LAP 34 - Throttle cable
P. CARINI	FERRARI	LAP 41 - Mechanical
E. de GRAFFENRIED	MASERATI	LAP 71 - Engine
F. BONETTO	MASERATI	LAP 78 - Out of fuel
A. ASCARI	FERRARI	LAP 80 - Spun off
O. MARIMON	MASERATI	LAP 80 - Collision

Chapter 3

BRITISH GRAND PRIX
17 JULY 1954

The Circuit

SILVERSTONE

90 laps of 4.7 KM

423 KM = 262.83 MILES

The R.A.C. showed great initiative in 1948 when they organised the first major motor-racing event in Britain after World War 2. Silverstone aerodrome was the venue for the British Grand Prix which was won by Luigi Villoresi (Maserati) but the large crowd—and the drivers—found the original figure-of-eight circuit rather slow and uninteresting.

The 2.9 mile converted airfield circuit soon became established and in 1952 the R.A.C. delegated authority to the B.R.D.C. to organise the event. Silverstone is not an ultra-fast circuit like Spa or Monza but is full of interest for spectators.

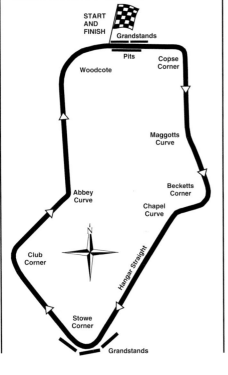

Starting Grid

S. MOSS	J. M. HAWTHORN	J. F. GONZALEZ	J. M. FANGIO
MASERATI	FERRARI	FERRARI	MERCEDES-BENZ
1.47	1.46	1.46	1.45

R. SALVADORI	K. KLING	J. BEHRA
MASERATI	MERCEDES-BENZ	GORDINI
1.48	1.48	1.48

P. COLLINS	B. BIRA	K. WHARTON	M. TRINTIGNANT
VANWALL SPECIAL	MASERATI	MASERATI	FERRARI
1.50	1.49	1.49	1.48

R. PARNELL	C. BUCCI	A. PILETTE
FERRARI	GORDINI	GORDINI
1.52	1.52	1.51

F. R. GERARD	D. BEAUMAN	H. SCHELL	R. MANZON
COOPER-BRISTOL	CONNAUGHT	MASERATI	FERRARI
1.55	1.55	1.53	1.52

J. R-PRICHARD	H. GOULD	W. WHITEHOUSE
CONNAUGHT	COOPER-BRISTOL	CONNAUGHT
1.58	1.56	1.56

E. BRANDON	P. WHITEHEAD	L. THORNE	L. MARR
COOPER	COOPER-ALTA	CONNAUGHT	CONNAUGHT
2.05	2.00	1.59	1.58

O. MARIMON	L. VILLORESI	A. BROWN
MASERATI	MASERATI	COOPER-BRISTOL
No practice time	No practice time	No practice time

R. MIERES	A. ASCARI	L. ROSIER
MASERATI	MASERATI	FERRARI
No practice time	No practice time	No practice time

NON - STARTER
A. BROWN
COOPER-BRISTOL

Revenge is Sweet

*I*n the summer of 1954, six months after the introduction of a new Formula 1 for Grand Prix cars which allowed a maximum capacity of $2\frac{1}{2}$ litres unsupercharged, Mercedes-Benz of Germany re-entered Grand Prix racing. Before the war, from 1934 to 1939, the German teams of Mercedes-Benz and Auto-Union had dominated the Grand Prix scene and the Germans staged their come-back with typical thoroughness.

They chose Juan Fangio, on the very top of his form, to lead the team and designed a revolutionary Grand Prix car with bodywork that was completely enveloping and fully streamlined. The power unit was a straight-eight, fuel-injection engine laid on its side at an angle in the chassis, so as to present a low overall height. And they chose the French Grand Prix of 1954, on the 150-mile-an-hour Rheims circuit, to race their new cars for the first time.

Their choice of a circuit could not have been better, for the streamlined cars pulverised the opposition and brought to an end the long run of Italian successes in Grand Prix racing since the war. Never in the history of motor-racing has a *marque* made such a sensational re-entry into the sport. Only six cars, and two of them were Mercedes-Benz, finished the race out of a field of twenty-one. Car after car blew up trying to maintain the blistering pace set by Mercedes-Benz, and the only driver who really gave the Germans a run for their money that day, before his Ferrari blew up on the thirteenth lap, was the thirty-two-year-old Argentine driver Froilan Gonzalez.

Following their overwhelming victory at Rheims, the Mercedes-Benz *équipe* left for England and the airfield circuit of Silverstone, determined to win the British Grand Prix, next round in the 1954 World Championship of Drivers. And it was at this stage that Froilan Gonzalez stepped into the picture again, but with far more satisfactory results than at Rheims.

From time to time in the varied, exciting history of motor-racing there emerges a driver who is a true entertainer. He may not be a potential world champion and he is possibly an untidy driver, lacking in style, but he never fails to stir the imagination of the crowds. Such a man was Gonzalez, a driver from the Argentine who was excitable to the point of quick temperedness and had a forceful driving style that was frequently alarming, so much like the antics of a bull in a china shop that it earned for him the title of 'The Prairie Bull'. By nature fiery and temperamental the chubby-faced, balding driver from Buenos Aires was as tough as nails and had the stamina of an ox. He was an ideal subject for nicknames—"Pepe", "Gonzo" and "The Puma" being but a few.

Gonzalez raced for the first time in 1946, in the Argentine, when he captured the hearts and imagination of his equally excitable countrymen, but it was not until 1950 that he pitted his skill against the European *pilotes*. He quickly became as popular with the European crowds as with his own countrymen. His vigorous style of driving was always worth watching; and although in 1951 his style, when he drove in the Ferrari team, was not quite that of the impeccable Guiseppe Farina who drove for Alfa-Romeo, his lap times were only a little slower than those of the 1950 world champion.

It is drivers like Gonzalez who can be relied upon to pull off the unexpected and completely upset the motor-racing scene at a time when it seems that a pattern has been set. He did just that in July 1951, humbling the all-powerful Alfa-Romeo team in the British Grand Prix at Silverstone and writing an epic chapter in motor-racing history.

The Alfa-Romeos had won every world championship event since the start of the previous season, but the opposition from Ferrari had been growing stronger. In the British Grand Prix, after a tremendous battle with Fangio's Alfa-Romeo, Gonzalez toppled Alfas from their pedestal and heralded not only the end of Alfa-Romeo supremacy but the emergence of himself as a top-flight driver.

Now, three years later, the 'Prairie Bull' was on form again. Could he shatter the myth of Mercedes-Benz invincibility as conclusively as he had humbled Alfa-Romeo in 1951? In Brackley, a country town a few miles from Silverstone, the arguments between enthusiasts waged fast and furious after the first practice session. In the wet—and there are few places more miserable when it is raining than a motor-racing circuit during practice—Mike Hawthorn's Ferrari put up fastest time. The young Englishman, very much at home at Silverstone, lapped the 2.9 mile airfield circuit in 2 min. 3 sec., an average speed of 85.67 m.p.h. Gonzalez was one second slower with his Ferrari, whilst Fangio could do not better than 2 min. 5 sec.

The streamlined German cars were proving a handful on the featureless airfield circuit, and the drivers were having difficulty judging the corners owing to the restricted view of their front wheels. It was obvious that Fangio and Kling, the two Mercedes drivers, would have felt much happier in conventional racing cars with open instead of enclosed front wheels. As it was, they were cutting in very close to the empty drums marking the line of the corners.

On Friday, the second day of practice, as though to prove the cars were not a handful, Fangio went out with only a minimum of fuel in the tank and with the considerably lightened car put in a tremendous lap at an average of 100.35 m.p.h. This was on a dry track, but even so it was the first time that one hundred miles an hour had been recorded at Silverstone by a $2^1/_2$ litre car.

Fangio's time of 1 min. 45 sec. was one second faster than Gonzalez and Hawthorn, and two seconds faster than Moss in his privately owned 250F Maserati. Fangio's progress round the circuit was frightening, for he was driving absolutely on the limit, and there were few people who saw him during this tremendous lap who did not have their heart in their mouth. When he pulled into the Mercedes pit it was obvious that he had been in trouble locating the marker drums, for the nearside front wing of the sleek, low Mercedes was badly dented. In fact he had written off quite a few drums during his meteoric lap. Gonzalez, on the other hand, had been taking things much easier and was well pleased with the way his Ferrari handled. Gonzalez fans were loud in their praise of the Argentine driver that night in Brackley. Pepe was going to be a hard man to beat next day, and there was no reason why he should not repeat his success of only two months previously at Silverstone when he won both heat and final at the International Trophy meeting.

On Saturday, from a very early hour, cars, coaches and motor-cycles converged on the Silverstone circuit from all directions. It was blustering and wet, but some enthusiasts had been there all night, so as to be sure of a good vantage point, and they were already cooking breakfast when the first early morning arrivals joined them.

There are other circuits—good circuits—but Silverstone is and always has been *the* circuit to the British motor-racing enthusiast. Soon, portable grandstands were being erected—the most ambitious ones in three or four sections with cover against the rain and a desk for lap charts and stop-watches. By the time the seat holders in the grandstands started to arrive, there were so many portable grandstands in the enclosures that, in parts, Silverstone looked like an African village on stilts.

After a sports-car race at 10.30 the Grand Prix cars were wheeled on to the starting grid at midday for the seventh British Grand Prix. The circuit had dried out and this was a relief to some drivers, but the atmosphere was not exactly a carefree one. The re-entry of Mercedes-Benz into Grand Prix racing had given the sport an intense do-or-die look and—as at Rheims—there was not very much laughter on the grid.

The Italians, absolutely supreme in motor-racing since the war, had another very good reason for looking serious. Their national pride had been severely mauled at

Rheims, and the British Grand Prix would give them an opportunity for revenge. And so, on an old World War 2 airfield in Northants, the scene was set for the second round in the struggle for supremacy between Mercedes-Benz of Germany and the red cars of Italy, and another round in the friendly rivalry between Fangio and Gonzalez.

It was sixteen years since Mercedes-Benz had last raced in England and nearly 100,000 spectators waited tensely around the circuit for the 'off'. Jammed against each other like sardines in a tin, the spectators on the balcony above the pits and the crowds in the grandstand watched as the cars were wheeled on to the grid.

Fangio's silver Mercedes was in pole position, nearest to the starter, then the Ferrari of Gonzalez, then Hawthorn's Ferrari and Moss's Maserati—painted in Britain's national motor-racing colour of green. On the second row was Salvadori's Maserati, Kling's Mercedes-Benz, and Behra with one of the French Gordinis. There were thirty-one cars in all, with the 'works' Maseratis of Ascari, Villoresi and Marimon at the back of the grid, having arrived too late for official practice.

Five minutes to go...four minutes...three...two. The seconds ticked by, every driver in his cockpit, and as an official held up a board '1 minute to go' German mechanics engaged a portable starter at the rear of each Mercedes and the eight-cylinder engines were suddenly alive. The harsh crackle of the Mercedes mingled with the more urgent blipping of the Ferraris and Maseratis. Then the grid was empty, except for thirty-one cars, each driver with his eyes on the starter as the flag was raised.

Ten seconds, five seconds and the high-pitched scream of the engines drowned all else. Like a moving carpet the whole grid seemed to edge forward and then the flag was down and they were away. At Copse it was an unnerving sight as the field swept towards the corner like a traffic jam gone mad, Gonzalez out in front and hunched over the wheel. As the Argentine driver went through Copse he had Moss, Hawthorn and Fangio sitting on his tail, waiting for the slightest error of judgment.

The starting grid was uncannily quiet. As the field swept round Silverstone on the first of ninety laps, commentators excitedly ticked off the progress of the leaders. 'They're coming down Hangar Straight to Stowe Corner—looks like a red car still in the lead.'

Sure enough it was Gonzalez who went through Stowe in front. Right again at Club Corner, left at Abbey Curve, and then the crowds in the grandstands could see the Ferrari. Gonzalez came through Woodcote Corner so fast it seemed that he must fly off to the left like a stone on the end of a string. And whilst we in the Press Box were wondering how on earth anyone could get through Woodcote at such a speed the trio of Hawthorn, Fangio and Moss came through just as fast, a series of high-pitched squeals from the protesting tyres accompanying their progress. Some pace, and it was heartening to see an Italian car out in front—the crowd loved it.

Fangio had other ideas. For ten minutes—four laps—he let Gonzalez and Hawthorn

M. F. Gonzalez, as tough as he looks and sometimes fiery and temperamental, had a forceful style of driving—often alarming—that earned him the of the 'Prairie Bull'. He raced the first time in Argentina in 1946, made a name for himself round the European circuits in 1950, won the British G.P. in 1, and was third in the World Championship table.
(Norman Newbatt)

A group of journalists and enthusiasts regard with undisguised admiration the two e W 196 Mercedes-Benz in the addock at Silverstone. Note the detatchable steering wheel on Kling's car.
(Norman Newbatt)

From the front row of the grid onzalez streaked into the lead, and held the lead for the entire race in spite of Fangio's erhuman efforts to catch him. onzalez drove a faultless race, oubled by showers towards the end. It was a great day for the 'Prairie Bull'.
(Geoffrey Goddard)

▲

Silverstone was totally unsuita
for the fully-streamlined Germ
cars. Neither Fangio nor Kling
could see their front wheels an
was almost impossible to place
car accurately on a corner.
Fangio clouted the marker dru
repeatedly.

(Norman Newbatt)

◄ Moss in his 250F Maserati lea
Hawthorn's Ferrari in a duel
awaited by enthusiasts. Moss l
at thirty laps, and at half dista
had built up a commanding le
Sadly, within ten laps of the fi
and with a 26 second lead ove
Hawthorn, Moss retired with r
axle trouble.

(Norman Newbatt)

When Gonzalez took the
chequered flag, having shown
clean pair of heels to everyone
else, he crossed the line 70 sec
ahead of Hawthorn.

(Norman Newbatt)

▼

stay out in front, and then on the fifth lap he took Hawthorn for second place and settled down grimly to whittle down the lead of five seconds that Gonzalez had built up. Just five seconds—not long on a watch face—but a commanding lead at Silverstone.

In five laps Fangio won back two seconds, but he had to work like a Trojan, and he sent the marker drums flying in all directions as well as taking to the grass verge more than once. As Fangio tried desperately to close the gap, Moss and Hawthorn were engaged in a tremendous struggle for third place, a struggle long awaited by British enthusiasts, for up to now Moss had not been able to race against Hawthorn on equal terms. In this race Moss had his recently acquired 250F Maserati, an even match for the 'works' Ferrari that Hawthorn was driving.

The sky was dark and overcast and rain was imminent. Gonzalez put on the pressure and turned in one electrifying lap of 1 min. 50 sec., an average speed of 95.79 m.p.h., which Fangio immediately equalled. With fifteen laps marked off on the lap charts, Fangio had managed—by a superhuman effort—to get to within one second of Gonzalez, whilst the battle between Moss and Hawthorn still raged.

When the rain came down, Gonzalez was in a much more favourable position than Fangio who now had to cope with blinding spray from the back wheels of the Ferrari. In fact the 'Prairie Bull' was certainly not throwing himself or his car about like a bull in a china shop as on previous occasions, and had no need to do so. The Mercedes was 'taped'. Fangio was fully extended and Gonzalez knew it.

With thirty laps completed—one third of the race distance—Gonzalez led Fangio by five seconds, whilst Moss led Hawthorn. In the cockpit of the Mercedes Fangio found that he no longer had third gear. The odds were certainly against him, but as on so many other occasions this simply had the effect of spurring Fangio on to even greater efforts. Other drivers would have dropped back but not Fangio, and at half distance the gap that separated the Ferrari and Mercedes was only three seconds, the race average 94.08 m.p.h.

The duel between the two British drivers had been won by Moss, and as Hawthorn's engine faltered, Moss increased the gap to ten seconds. Then Moss, never more brilliant than when taking up the chase, went after Fangio. The seconds were lopped off in pairs, and suddenly Moss was closing right up on the Mercedes. Next time round, with fifty-five laps completed, the Englishman led, and a full-throated cheer greeted the Maserati as it came through Woodcote Corner and past the stands. Three laps later, with two thirds of the race completed, Hawthorn also passed Fangio. With Italian cars in the first three places—driven by an Argentine and two Englishmen—it should at least be a partial Italian victory to avenge Rheims.

Out in front, as is so often the case when the leader is driving a cool, calculated race on the very top of his form—the magnificent performance of Gonzalez went almost unnoticed. He had to watch Moss, who was only eighteen seconds behind at seventy laps, but it was obvious that 'Pepe' was keeping just that little extra in reserve.

By now the gap between Gonzalez and Fangio had widened to fifty-three seconds, but still Fangio refused to give in. He drove the Mercedes just as fast and as hard as he could—in spite of the rain, in spite of having no third gear, and in spite of the difficulty of sighting the German car in relation to the position of the drums. By now the battered front of the Mercedes, after a series of collisions with the marker drums, looked a sorry sight. And then fate took a hand yet again as the cockpit of the Mercedes filled with fumes. Fangio, his eyes smarting, could do nothing to counter this final devastating blow. With twelve laps still to be run, the Mercedes dropped back and Marimon moved up into fourth place with his Maserati.

There was more drama yet to come. With eighty of the ninety laps completed, and with a lead of twenty-six seconds over Hawthorn, the unlucky Moss was missing when the field came through Woodcote. There was Gonzalez, then a lengthy gap of almost a minute, then Hawthorn, but no sign of Moss. Shortly afterwards he arrived at the pits having abandoned the car out on the circuit. Later, his mechanic, Alf Francis, found that one of the reduction gears in the rear axle had become loose and slipped off its splined shaft. It was wretched luck but Moss had beaten Mike Hawthorn fairly and squarely and that was sufficient reward for one day.

There was no more drama. Gonzalez continued to go round and round as though his Ferrari was on rails and he took the chequered flag seventy seconds ahead of Hawthorn's Ferrari; Marimon was third (so it was still Italian cars one...two...three) and Fangio finished fourth.

The Germans had been beaten, and the smiling, chubby-faced Gonzalez had led the race throughout like a world champion and evened the score at one all—Rheims to the Germans, Silverstone to the Italians. But what a magnificent fight Fangio had made of it. Only he could have coped with so much misfortune in one afternoon, and his superhuman efforts almost overshadowed the masterly performance of Froilan Gonzalez—but not quite.

Results
90 Laps

1.	J.F. GONZALEZ	FERRARI	2 HR 56 MIN 14.0 SEC
			144.34 KPH (89.69 MPH)
2.	J.M. HAWTHORN	FERRARI	2 HR 57 MIN 24.0 SEC
3.	O. MARIMON	MASERATI	89 LAPS
4.	J.M. FANGIO	MERCEDES-BENZ	89 LAPS
5.	M. TRINTIGNANT	FERRARI	87 LAPS
6.	R. MIERES	MASERATI	87 LAPS
7.	K. KLING	MERCEDES-BENZ	87 LAPS
8.	K. WHARTON	MASERATI	86 LAPS
9.	A. PILETTE	GORDINI	86 LAPS
10.	F.R. GERARD	COOPER-BRISTOL	85 LAPS
11.	D. BEAUMAN	CONNAUGHT	84 LAPS
12.	H. SCHELL	MASERATI	83 LAPS
13.	L. MARR	CONNAUGHT	82 LAPS
14.	L. THORNE	CONNAUGHT	78 LAPS
15.	H. GOULD	COOPER-BRISTOL	44 LAPS

FASTEST LAP: J.F. GONZALEZ (FERRARI), **J.M. HAWTHORN** (FERRARI),
O. MARIMON (MASERATI), **J.M. FANGIO** (MERCEDES-BENZ),
S. MOSS (MASERATI), **J. BEHRA** (GORDINI), **A. ASCARI** (MASERATI)
ALL IN **1 MIN 50.0 SEC** AT **154.159 KPH** (95.79 MPH).

Retirements

E. BRANDON	COOPER	Lap 3
L. ROSIER	FERRARI	LAP 3 - Engine
P. WHITEHEAD	COOPER-ALTA	LAP 5 - Oil pipe
R. MANZON	FERRARI	LAP 16 - Cracked block
P. COLLINS	VANWALL SPECIAL	LAP 17 - Gasket
C. BUCCI	GORDINI	LAP 18 - Accident
A. ASCARI	MASERATI	LAP 21 - Valve
R. PARNELL	FERRARI	LAP 26 - Engine
J. RISELEY-PRICHARD	CONNAUGHT	LAP 41 - Accident
L. VILLORESI/A. ASCARI	MASERATI	LAP 41 - Connecting rod
B. BIRA	MASERATI	LAP 45 - Accident
R. SALVADORI	MASERATI	LAP 54 - Transmission
J. BEHRA	GORDINI	LAP 55 - Rear suspension
W. WHITEHOUSE	CONNAUGHT	LAP 64 - Engine
S. MOSS	MASERATI	LAP 80 - Rear axle

Chapter 4

*ARGENTINE GRAND PRIX
16 JANUARY 1955*

The Circuit

BUENOS AIRES

96 Laps of 3.912 KM

375.55 KM = 233.35 MILES

In the Argentine Grand Prix of 1955—an unbelievably gruelling race in a heatwave for three exhausting hours—Juan Fangio drove his Mercedes-Benz for 96 laps without a change of car. The 2.43 mile artificial road circuit No. 2 of the Buenos Aires Autodrome is not particularly fast but it is an exacting circuit which has only one fast straight of any length and numerous twists and turns. The circuit has modern pit installations, vast covered stands, and large open enclosures. Spectator capacity is 300,000. When the cars were wheeled on to the grid it was 100°F., and the track temperature was around 135, with humidity at 23%. Few drivers could stand the searing heat in the cockpit for one hour, let alone three, and yet Fangio seemed unperturbed as he reeled off the laps and won a well deserved victory.

Starting Grid

J. BEHRA	**J. M. FANGIO**	**A. ASCARI**	**J. F. GONZALEZ**
MASERATI	MERCEDES-BENZ	LANCIA	FERRARI
1.43.8	**1.43.6**	**1.43.6**	**1.43.1**

H. SCHELL	**K. KLING**	**G. FARINA**
MASERATI	MERCEDES-BENZ	FERRARI
1.44.3	**1.44.1**	**1.43.8**

L. VILLORESI	**H. HERRMANN**	**P. BIRGER**	**S. MOSS**
LANCIA	MERCEDES-BENZ	GORDINI	MERCEDES-BENZ
1.45.2	**1.44.8**	**1.44.8**	**1.44.4**

M. TRINTIGNANT	**C. MENDITEGUY**	**E. CASTELLOTTI**
FERRARI	MASERATI	LANCIA
1.45.8	**1.45.4**	**1.45.3**

L. MUSSO	**J. IGLESIAS**	**R. MIERES**	**E. BAYOL**
MASERATI	GORDINI	MASERATI	GORDINI
1.46.5	**1.46.4**	**1.46.3**	**1.46.1**

A. URIA	**C. BUCCI**	**S. MANTOVANI**
MASERATI	MASERATI	MASERATI
1.51.2	**1.48.8**	**1.47.6**

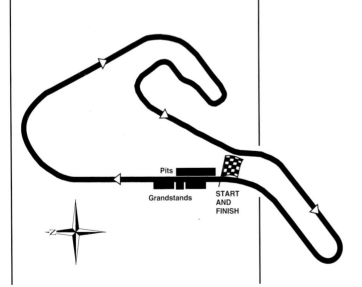

Pits

Grandstands

START
AND
FINISH

Heatwave in Argentina

Fangio

O f all the events counting towards the annual World Championship of Drivers, none is more likely to produce high drama or the unexpected than the Argentine Grand Prix. No country has ever been more enthusiastic about motor-racing—not even Italy; and in 1953, as a tribute to those two great Argentine drivers, Juan Fangio (world champion in 1951) and Froilan Gonzalez, the Argentine Grand Prix was given world championship status. The Argentine had become a force to be reckoned with in the world of motor-racing.

The 1953 Grand Prix took place in January and was run over the brand new Buenos Aires Autodrome, a fine—if small—artificial road circuit with modern pit installations, vast stands in the nature of a football stadium and huge enclosures. Up till now it had been inter-city stock-car racing, over thousands of miles, that had captured the imagination of the Argentine crowds. Races like the Grand Prix Del Norte—from Buenos Aires across the Plains and over the Andes to Lima in Peru and back again. Today's race, on a closed circuit, was different for it ranked with the most important classics on the international calendar.

It was no surprise when half a million people turned out to see the opening world championship event of 1953, the first of a series of duels between the Italian teams of Ferrari and Maserati. The Ferraris were driven by Villoresi (winner of the Buenos Aires or Argentine Grand Prix in 1947 and 1948) and by the 1949 winner, Ascari, supported by Farina and Hawthorn. The Maseratis were in the hands of Fangio and Gonzalez, Argentine's own drivers, supported by Galvez and Bonetto. The thousands who streamed out to the Autodrome eagerly awaited the outcome of the duel between their two national idols, Fangio and Gonzalez, in this first world championship event to be held in Argentina.

It was no surprise—not to the Argentine enthusiasts, anyway—when thousands of spectators swarmed on to the track to greet General Peron, bowling over the police like ninepins and fiercely resisting every measure to get them back behind the safety barriers again. Many of them stayed on the edge of the track until the start, some of them remained there whilst the race was in progress and occasionally a particularly enthusiastic spectator would risk his life by rushing from one side of the track to the other in search of a better vantage point.

Mike Hawthorn raced a Ferrari for the first time in the 1953 Argentine Grand Prix and was amazed by the lack of crowd control. On his return to England he described how on the thirty-second lap a spectator ran across the track in front of Farina's Ferrari. The Italian driver swerved violently and shot off the track at a tangent—into the crowd. Fifteen people died, many more were injured. Then an ambulance, on the way to the scene of the accident and driven flat out by an Argentine driver, killed two more spectators. This was not all: a mounted policeman who was unwise enough to use a whip to control the wildly enthusiastic crowds on one part of the circuit was dragged from his horse and beaten to death. Hawthorn was more than glad when the race was over. The race...? It was won by Ascari, with Villoresi second and Gonzalez third. Fangio retired with transmission trouble.

The Argentine Grand Prix of 1954 provided more drama. Once again it opened the world championship season; once again hundreds of thousands of fans filled the Autodrome to capacity, and once again the crowds were more interested in the outcome of the duel between Fangio and Gonzalez than in which team was victorious.

This was the first world championship event to be run in accordance with the new Formula 1—a maximum engine capacity of $2\frac{1}{2}$ litres unsupercharged—and there were four Argentine drivers of note: Fangio, Gonzalez, Fangio's protégé Marimon, and Mieres. The European opposition came from Farina, Hawthorn and Trintignant.

Fangio, with a Maserati, gave one of the finest displays of driving the knowledgeable Argentine crowd had ever seen. In torrential rain and on a track waterlogged at times he was complete master of the situation. When the rain eased, the Ferraris driven by Gonzalez and Hawthorn closed on the Maserati, but then the heavens opened again and Fangio pulled away. It was an incredible performance and as the weather worsened he gained even more ground.

On lap 64 Fangio pulled into the pits and as Farina went by into the lead the wheels of the Maserati were changed for a set with more suitable rain tyres. Some say that only three mechanics (the regulation number) worked on Fangio's car whilst others, including the Ferrari team manager Ugolini, maintained that five Maserati mechanics changed the wheels.

Ugolini was sure of his ground and lodged a protest, so convinced that Fangio would be disqualified that he slowed down Farina, which allowed Fangio to streak by into the lead again. Farina was not sorry, for the rain at this time was coming down in buckets, but he took another view entirely when Fangio was given the chequered flag and it was announced that the Argentine driver had *not* been disqualified. The ensuing argument between an absolutely livid Farina and Ugolini will long be remembered by those who witnessed it.

And so, with a reputation for drama and incident, the Argentine Grand Prix of 1955 once again opened the world championship season. Run in a fierce heatwave on January 16th, over ninety-six laps of the 2.43 mile circuit, it was one of the most fantastic motor-races in the history of the sport. Of the twenty-one drivers who lined up on the starting grid for this gruelling race only one drove his car for the whole ninety-six laps—without collapsing from the heat or handing over his car to another driver—and that was Juan Fangio.

It was obvious as soon as the first practice session opened that it was going to be a race in which stamina would be more important than the performance of the car or the ability of the driver. Stirling Moss, a great believer in physical fitness and with tremendous reserves of stamina, summed up the feelings of the European *équipes*: 'It is impossible to drive three hours in this heat.'

One can understand Moss's feelings. The Mercedes team—including Moss who had just been signed on—left Stuttgart wearing overcoats, when the temperature was 73°F. When they alighted from their plane at Buenos Aires it was like opening the door of a furnace: the temperature was 104 in the shade! In ten years, so said the locals, it had never been so hot in January.

The townsfolk of Buenos Aires cooled off in the roadside bars and cafés, conserving just sufficient energy to argue about the relative merits of the drivers and cars. Cafés in the vicinity of the junction of Avenida Corrientes and Avenida of July 9th were more crowded than most, for the large obelisk in the middle of the road carried enormous photographic enlargements of the drivers and their cars. And above the portraits fluttered the flags of all the nations that compete in international motor sport.

Any driver unwise enough to show himself was immediately mobbed by the crowd as though he were a teenage idol, and loud-speakers kept up a continuous barrage, reminding the already wildly excited Argentine enthusiasts that the world's best drivers would be at the Autodrome on January 16th.

Understandably, the talk was mainly of Fangio and Gonzalez, but there was something else almost as interesting to discuss. For the first time since 1947, when the Maseratis and Alfa-Romeos from Europe first raced in the Argentine and motor-racing became a national sport, Mercedes-Benz were challenging the supremacy of Italian cars. And it was their own Fangio who led the German team, supported by Stirling Moss and two German drivers—Kling and Herrmann.

Gonzalez led the Ferrari team, supported by Farina and Trintignant, with Maglioli as spare driver. Farina was racing for the first time since an accident during a practice session at Monza in June of the previous year when he had been severely burned and had since been given more than a hundred skin graftings.

The Maserati team of five cars was led by Frenchman Jean Behra and included Schell, Mantovani, Mieres and Musso, whilst three V.8 Lancias were in the hands of Ascari (winner of the Argentine Classic in 1953), Castellotti and Villoresi.

It was the second Grand Prix appearance of the Lancias following their début in the Spanish Grand Prix in October 1954 when Ascari put up a most impressive performance—with fastest lap in practice and during the race—before retiring with clutch trouble after only ten laps. The Lancias's acceleration out of the corners and its high maximum speed created a sensation, but there appeared to be considerable room for improvement in road holding.

It was the most formidable opposition that either Fangio or Gonzalez had ever faced in the Argentine.

In the week before the race that overworked, underpaid but nevertheless enthusiastic body of men—the racing mechanics—slaved on the cars, getting them ready in the oven-like heat of garages for the first qualifying trials. The betting in Buenos Aires was in favour of Mercedes in spite of the fact that the German cars did not appear to be as fast as the Ferraris or Lancias. There was, in fact, a certain amount of very spirited criticism of the German cars from followers of the Italian *équipes* who maintained that they were slow in acceleration out of the turns, that they had inadequate brakes, and that their roadholding was poor. Finally, it was argued, no one could stand the heat in the cockpit of a Mercedes for one hour, let alone three.

The qualifying trials told a different story. Admittedly Gonzalez was fastest with a time of 1 min. 43.1 sec., but Fangio and Ascari were only five-tenths of a second slower. Fangio was quite unconcerned about the criticism of Mercedes-Benz. He was far more worried about the heat, well aware of the fact that every driver was going to need to be at the peak of his mental and physical fitness to even last the course, let alone win the race.

The fourth position on the front row went to Behra's Maserati with a time of 1 min. 43.8 sec. and thus there were four different *marques* of car on the front row, a line-up that promised a closely fought race.

On race day some 300,000 spectators made their way to the Autodrome. They could talk of nothing else but the Grand Prix and so as to be sure of a seat in the main grandstand, or in one of the capacious stands out in the open under the full heat of the

welcome, cooling shower for Fangio during a practice session.
(Mercedes Benz AG) ▶

▶

No cooling shower on race day as the four Mercedes-Benz are pushed to the starting grid. The temperature was already 96° F. in the shade , with the track temperature around 140° F.
(Mercedes-Benz AG)

Fangio (Mercedes) has a slight advantage over Ascari (Lancia) as they take off from the front row of the grid. The Lancias proved very fast but all three had been eliminated in crashes by quarter distance.
▼ **(Mercedes-Benz AG)**

ss appears to be gasping for
ath in the blistering heat
he Mercedes cockpit.
adrant/Autocar

▲ *A puzzled Moss, who pulled o*
circuit after thirty laps, with
vapour lock in the fuel lines,
explain that he is not sufferin
from sunstroke, and it is the
that needs attention. Unconv
the marshals bundled him in
ambulance and it was some
before he was able to get back
the circuit where he took over
Kling.
(Mercedes-Benz AG)

CENTRE LEFT: Fangio and M
typical Mercedes 1-2 formatio
During this gruelling race—b
and after the fuel pump failu
Moss fully justified his place i
German team. Never one to q
whatever the odds, Moss was
determined to finish his first r
for Mercedes-Benz—and did
(National Motor Museum)

◄

Fangio raises his gloved hand
victory salute. He was the only
driver to keep going from star
finish, without driver relief, fo
full race distance of 233 miles
(Mercedes-Benz AG)

sun, most of them had arrived by ten o'clock, in time for bicycle races, motor-cycle races and a display of aerial acrobatics that whetted their appetite for what was to come.

The Grand Prix was due to start at 4 p.m. and at 3.30—in tropical heat—the twenty-one cars were wheeled on to the grid. The German cars looked most odd with gaping holes cut in the bodywork for cooling purposes and heat deflectors fitted over the exhaust pipes. It was nearly 100 degrees in the shade (but there was no shade for the drivers) and the ground temperature was 131. The air had a humidity content of twenty-three per cent!

A few seconds before 4 p.m. the flag was raised. The engine note grew shriller, one or two cars at the rear of the grid started to edge forward and then the field was away, Fangio out in front to the confusion of his critics, Gonzalez on his tail. Then, in a bunch, Ascari, Moss, Kling, Schell, Behra and Farina.

For two laps Fangio held the lead round this twisting, exacting circuit which has only one straight of any length where the cars can reach their maximum speed. On the second lap a chapter of incidents started to unfold that was one of constant drama until the race ended at 7 p.m.—three exhausting hours later. Behra entered a bend too fast in his Maserati and spun. Schell, in another Maserati, swerved on to the grass between Behra and the crowded enclosures on the corner. Kling's Mercedes hit Behra's car and careered off the track.

The Mercedes demolished a fence and Kling finally brought the car to a stop less than six feet from the wire safety barrier guarding the spectators. Meanwhile Behra's car had been rammed by Birger's Gordini and, in braking hard, Birger had been rammed by Menditeguy's Maserati. Just for good measure, and whilst Behra was wondering what was going to hit him next, Villoresi lost control of his Lancia and ran off the track.

The result of all this, after less than six minutes of racing, was that five drivers were already out: Kling, Behra, Villoresi, Menditeguy and Birger.

By now Ascari had wrested the lead from Fangio. The master tactician, whose race plan was to avoid becoming involved in any duels during the opening laps, was quite content to let someone else set the pace at this stage of the race, particularly as that someone soon had Gonzalez sitting on his tail. With any luck, mused Fangio, these two old protagonists would tire themselves out. The cockpit of the Mercedes was already like an oven.

On the sixth lap Gonzalez went rocketing by into the lead, urging his car forward in characteristic fashion to the delight of the spectators. The order was then Gonzalez (Ferrari), Ascari (Lancia), Fangio (Mercedes), Moss (Mercedes) and Schell (Maserati). At this stage Behra decided to re-enter the fray and took over Mantovani's Maserati.

With ten laps completed, the race average was 78.564 m.p.h., and two minutes later

Ascari went by Gonzalez like an express train and proceeded to pull away from the burly Argentine driver. Now, with less than an eighth of the race completed, the heat claimed its first victim. Castellotti retired with sunstroke and Villoresi took over the Lancia. Out on the circuit every driver was slowly grilling in the cockpit, sweating freely, peering into the heat haze as the circuit seemed, momentarily, to turn in the wrong direction. Heat can play queer tricks with tired eyes.

With twenty-one laps completed, Ascari still led, followed by Gonzalez, Fangio and Moss. By now the heat had claimed another victim—the plucky Farina, his left leg (burned in the crash at Monza) encased in asbestos to protect it from the cockpit heat. He handed his car over to Maglioli, Ferrari's spare driver. A few seconds later Ascari lost control of his Lancia at a fast right-hand bend and crashed into the fence. The world champion of 1952 and 1953 shook his head sadly and climbed out unhurt. Now only one Lancia was left of the three that had started and it seemed certain there was something radically wrong with the roadholding of the Turin cars.

Ascari, his thin cotton vest saturated with sweat, and his trousers sticking to his legs and thighs with perspiration, walked disgustedly away from the car. Ignoring the warning, then the command of two policemen, he crossed the track and returned to the pits. His race was run.

Gonzalez led now, but only for another four laps. The heat claimed him as a sunstroke victim and the burly Argentine driver was lucky not to crash when his car ran off the track. Sickened by the heat and fumes, Gonzalez drove slowly round to the pits, and as Farina clambered gamely into the cockpit of the Ferrari, Froilan Gonzalez went out like a light. As Farina accelerated away, young Mantovani came into the pits and collapsed—exhausted. His car was taken over by Musso.

Now Fangio led once more, and Moss—anxious to put up a good show in his first race for the German team—lay second, some twelve seconds behind. For just under an hour Moss had sweated it out in the blistering heat of the Mercedes cockpit, matching Fangio's physical endurance with his own. Never one to quit, he was determined to finish the race.

Then fate took a hand. With only a third of the race distance of ninety-six laps completed, Moss pulled off the track with a vapour lock in the fuel lines. This was as good a time as any to relax so he eased himself on to the edge of the cockpit, sat there for a moment or two with his head resting on his hands, then got out of the car and lay full length on the ground. Moss was pretty well whacked—a most unusual sight.

Suddenly, whilst he was quietly minding his own business, a team of ambulance men pounced on him, bundled him into an ambulance and started off at breakneck speed, siren wailing. The ambulance men thought Moss had sunstroke and each time he raised himself to protest that he was quite O.K., and that it was the car that needed attention, they pushed him back. This wasn't funny. Moss made one last despairing effort and somehow or other he managed to get the message over—he was O.K., would they please stop their own private motor-race and get him back to his. This they did with profuse apologies.

Out at the Autodrome Fangio lay third, having stopped at his pit for three minutes for fuel, refreshment, and a welcome drenching with gallons of water poured over him. The stop let Schell's Maserati through into the lead, followed by the Maserati of Mieres, the Argentine driver.

Fangio had no intention of letting Schell keep the lead too long, but he need not have worried. On the fortieth lap Schell pulled into the pits, absolutely exhausted, and literally fell out of the car as Behra took over. Three laps later Mieres had to call in at the pits with a faulty petrol pump—and Fangio led again.

Mieres drove a masterly race that day and with Fangio was the only driver to keep going from start to finish without relief. He only completed ninety-one laps, five less than Fangio, but the faulty petrol pump cost him ten vital minutes, equivalent to six laps. He might well have won the race for Maserati but for this unfortunate pit stop. By this time only nine cars out of twenty-one starters were left in the race and not one Lancia remained. Villoresi, driving Castellotti's car, had run head on into a wall on lap thirty-six, luckily without serious injury.

By half distance, with one and a half hours still to go, Fangio held a commanding lead and on the forty-fifth lap this incredible driver, seemingly impervious to the heat, recorded fastest time of the day and tore round the Autodrome in 1 min. 48.3 sec., equal to 80.809 m.p.h. The heat in the cockpit of the Mercedes was so intense that Fangio sustained second-degree burns on the right leg during his fantastic drive, and the steering-wheel was almost too hot to hold. Few, if any, drivers would have carried on but the idol of the Argentine crowds refused to be beaten.

By now those drivers still left on the circuit were so exhausted that even gear changing was an effort and restricted to a minimum number of changes per lap. The pits area was like a casualty clearing station, with drivers lying exhausted in the shade of the pit counter as mechanics and others tried to bring them round.

Now Gonzalez reappeared on the scene in his own car—the one that Farina had taken over when Gonzalez collapsed in the early stages of the race. Farina had driven it until the thirty-eighth lap when he collapsed, and the car had been taken over by Trintignant who had delighted the crowd by pulling into the pits at regular intervals so that his mechanic could pour the contents of a bucket of water over him.

Now Gonzalez was once again intent on catching Fangio. He had not set himself an impossible task for the Ferrari was definitely faster than the Mercedes on this twisting circuit and Gonzalez was cutting back Fangio's lead at the rate of three to five seconds a lap. If he could keep up this merciless pace he could catch Fangio but shortly afterwards—soon after six o'clock—Gonzalez spun off the road at the exit from a tricky downhill bend. Once again the heat had proved too much for him and this time he retired for good. Once again the plucky Farina took over the car.

It was an almost unreal situation. The Ferrari were undoubtedly faster than the Mercedes yet unable to challenge the German car because their drivers lacked the almost superhuman stamina of Fangio.

At about this time Kling brought in the Mercedes he had taken over from Herrmann at half-distance when the young German driver had collapsed, and when he stopped the Mercedes at the pits it was as much as he could do to climb out of the cockpit. Of the drivers in the German team only Moss was left, apart from Fangio. Neubauer, the Mercedes-Benz team manager, ordered him to take over from Kling, and so once more Moss was in the race and he kept going until the finish.

The minutes ran out and still Fangio held on to the lead. Farina tried to carry on where Gonzalez had left off and succeeded in closing the gap a little, but Fangio had nearly two minutes in hand and there was just not time for the gallant Italian to catch the Mercedes.

As Fangio crossed the line is it any wonder that he waved both hands in the air to acknowledge the roar of applause from his countrymen. For he had not only won his country's classic race but he had broken the sequence of Italian victories since 1947 and defeated a three-pronged attack from Italy's Ferraris, Maseratis and Lancias by sheer guts and determination.

The table of results was almost farcical. Of the five cars still running at the end of the race, in addition to Fangio and Mieres, three had been driven by three different drivers and the other two by two different drivers.

On that sweltering January day Juan Fangio displayed to the maximum every one of the qualities that go to make the greatest racing drivers; strategy, skill, courage and dogged determination. The Argentine Grand Prix of 1955 was without a doubt Fangio's personal triumph.

Results
96 Laps

1.	**J.M. FANGIO**	MERCEDES-BENZ	**3 HR 0 MIN 38.6 SEC**
			124.738 KPH (77.508 MPH)
2.	**J.F. GONZALEZ/G. FARINA**		
	M. TRINTIGNANT/		
	J.F. GONZALEZ/G. FARINA	FERRARI	**3 HR 2 MIN 8.2 SEC**
3.	**G. FARINA/U. MAGLIOLI**		
	M. TRINTIGNANT/		
	U. MAGLIOLI	FERRARI	**94 LAPS**
4.	**H. HERRMANN/**		
	K. KLING/S. MOSS	MERCEDES-BENZ	**94 LAPS**
5.	**R. MIERES**	MASERATI	**91 LAPS**
6.	**H. SCHELL/J. BEHRA**	MASERATI	**88 LAPS**
7.	**L. MUSSO/H. SCHELL**	MASERATI	**83 LAPS**

FASTEST LAP: **J.M. FANGIO** (MERCEDES-BENZ) ON LAP 45
1 MIN 48.3 SEC AT **130.050 KPH (80.809 MPH)**

Retirements

L. VILLORESI	LANCIA	**LAP 2 - Damaged fuel Line**
J. BEHRA	MASERATI	**LAP 2 - Multiple accident**
P. BIRGER	GORDINI	**LAP 2 - Multiple accident**
K. KLING	MERCEDES-BENZ	**LAP 2 - Multiple accident**
C. MENDITEGUY	MASERATI	**LAP 2 - Multiple accident**
E. BAYOL	GORDINI	**LAP 8 - Transmission**
A. ASCARI	LANCIA	**LAP 22- Crashed**
A. URIA	MASERATI	**LAP 23 - Fuel starvation**
S. MOSS	MERCEDES-BENZ	**LAP 30 - Fuel lines vapour lock**
E. CASTELLOTTI/L. VILLORESI	LANCIA	**LAP 36 - Accident**
M. TRINTIGNANT	FERRARI	**LAP 37 - Broken valve**
J. IGLESIAS	GORDINI	**LAP 39 - Transmission**
C. BUCCI/C. MENDITEGUY/		
H. SCHELL	MASERATI	**LAP 56 - Out of fuel**
S. MANTOVANI/J. BEHRA/		
L. MUSSO	MASERATI	**LAP 56 - Fuel starvation**

Chapter 5

22nd MILLE MIGLIA
1–2 MAY 1955

The Circuit

BRESCIA-ROME-BRESCIA
ITALY
998 MILES

The Mille Miglia, since it was first run in 1927, has earned the reputation of being one of the most controversial races in the International Calendar.

This gruelling race, from Brescia to Rome and back over a thousand miles of good, bad, and indifferent roads is controversial because of the physical impossibility of adequately policing the route and controlling the vast crowds. It is estimated that five million spectators gather in cities, towns and villages along the route—as well as in the open country where the most powerful cars reach speeds approaching 170 miles an hour on the fast stretches. In the 1955 race the Moss/Jenkinson Mercedes-Benz averaged 98.53 mph for 10 hours 7 minutes, whilst a 500 cc Citroen took $18\frac{1}{2}$ hours to complete the course. In the mountains, competitors have to tackle passes like the Futa, the Radicofani and the Raticosa where the sinuous nature of the interminable climbs and descents exacts a heavy toll on average speeds. Admittedly the route is closed to normal everyday traffic, but the faster cars—which are last away from Brescia—have to pass scores of slower cars en route, often at speeds of well over one hundred miles per hour on narrow roads. Crowd control is impossible and spectators surge forward into the road for a better view.

One Thousand Miles Against the Clock

Grimy but jubilant, his face smeared with dust and grease, the young driver with the initials S.M. sewn on his white overalls above the badge of the British Racing Drivers' Club climbed thankfully out of the Mercedes-Benz sports car. With his bearded companion, motor-racing journalist Denis Jenkinson, Moss had just won the Mille Miglia—a race considered by many to be the toughest in the world.

For just over ten hours, practically non-stop and at an incredible average speed of 98.53 m.p.h., Moss drove the Mercedes-Benz to its limit over a thousand miles of the gruelling Mille Miglia course from Brescia to Rome and back again. His triumph, on a German car, in one of the most difficult, thrilling and dangerous events on the international calendar set Moss high on a pedestal, for he had wrested victory at record speed from Italian cars and drivers for the first time in nine years and—more important—became the first Englishman to win the Mille Miglia since it was originally run in 1927. And for good measure he had disproved a famous legend 'He who leads at Rome never leads at Brescia'—for Moss had led at Rome, and won.

Stirling Moss, twenty-five at the time, was able to write this glorious chapter of motor-racing history because of the detailed plan of action that he and Jenkinson worked out together; that, coupled with the meticulous preparation of his car by Mercedes-Benz, and his own superb driving ability.

In 1955 he was under contract to Mercedes-Benz for Grand Prix and sports car racing but he stood very little chance of winning any Grand Prix for his task was to shadow Juan Fangio, the No. 1 Mercedes driver. The Mille Miglia was different—a sports car race in which it was every man for himself. There were four Mercedes-Benz entries— Fangio, Moss, Kling and Herrmann—but there was absolutely no question of racing the cars as a team. In this classic event the competitors leave Brescia at one minute intervals and the driver who completes the course in the shortest time is the winner. It is as simple as that—a race against the clock.

The Mille Miglia (banned after The Marquis Alfonso de Portago crashed into a group of spectators at 150 m.p.h. in the 1957 race, killing himself, his co-driver Ed Nelson, and ten spectators) was run in 1955 over 1,000 miles of roads normally used by everyday traffic—the best and the worst of Italian roads. Traffic was of course banned for the duration of the race but there was no way of controlling the hundreds of thousands of wildly enthusiastic spectators who lined the towns and villages en route and commandeered vantage points in the mountains hours, and sometimes days, before the cars were due.

For the 1955 race Stirling Moss asked Jenkinson to accompany him as passenger, and these two then worked out an ingenious plan. They reasoned that the only way to win the race was to learn the thousand mile route so thoroughly that they could keep up a faster average than their Italian rivals, many of whom had a thorough knowledge of certain sections of the route but none of whom knew the whole route.

They acknowledged the fact that it was not humanly possible to put in many practice laps over a route that took two days in a touring car—two hazardous days with normal traffic on the roads. Even so, Alfred Neubauer—team manager of Mercedes-Benz—insisted that his drivers covered the route five times—5,000 miles in all—and Kling, one of his drivers, actually logged 30,000 miles in practice.

Most non-Italian teams train for the Mille Miglia on the theory that as it is impossible to learn the entire course of a thousand miles it is better to utilise the time at the team's disposal to learn certain of the more difficult sections of the route thoroughly. Neubauer's decision was undoubtedly a revolutionary one, and Moss and Jenkinson then decided to supplement it. They would log the entire 1,000 mile route.

In February, nearly three months before the race, Moss and Jenkinson made their first reconnaissance. Sheet after sheet of paper was filled in with such details as the severity and direction of corners, the length of straights where maximum speeds in the region of 170 m.p.h. were possible even when visibility was restricted, what lay on the far side of blind brows and blind hills, how fast every level-crossing and bridge could be taken, the severity of gradients, the direction of flat-out curves, and sections of the route such as a bumpy surface or tramlines where the car would be damaged unless speed was reduced.

Kilometre stones and easily visible landmarks were used to identify the mass of entries, and after Moss and Jenkinson had completed their third reconnaissance there were eighteen pages of notes, some a little difficult to read as they had been written at 150 m.p.h. Then a system of hand signals was devised so that Jenkinson could pass on the information to Moss during the race, for it would be quite impossible to converse in the noisy, open cockpit of the Mercedes.

The pages of notes were then converted into a single roll of continuous information—eighteen feet long—rather as though someone had typed on a toilet roll, and accommodated in an oblong, alloy case with a perspex-covered opening on the top. The roll of notes was held in the box by rollers, like a film spool in a camera, and by winding the notes from the lower roller to the upper one Jenkinson was able to read them through the perspex window. The mechanical brain was ready.

Every piece of information in the brain had to be absolutely correct, for both Moss and Jenkinson knew what would happen if, for instance, Jenkinson read the route and indicated a flat-out brow with a straight section on the far side when in fact the road turned left or right after the brow. Moss had got to trust Jenkinson and the mechanical brain implicitly at speeds up to 170 m.p.h. when the slightest error could mean disaster.

Whilst they had been perfecting the brain, Mercedes-Benz had been preparing the cars with their usual thoroughness. Apart from the fact that the power units were of course tuned to the utmost degree of perfection, the seats were made to measure for each driver and the pedals positioned with the same meticulous care. Nothing was too much trouble. The driver had got to be happy with the car. Finally, all was ready and the four Mercedes-Benz sports-racing cars were driven from Stuttgart to Brescia in the very rapid Mercedes transporters.

At 9 p.m. on Saturday May 1st the first of the small cars left the starting ramp at Brescia. At intervals of one minute the Renaults and Fiats accelerated away between the densely packed crowds lining the route. With over five hundred cars to send off, it would be morning before the powerful Mercedes and Ferraris left Brescia, so Moss and Jenkinson slept through the night. At 6.30 they reported to Neubauer at the Control and twenty-five minutes later the first sports car of over 2-litre capacity accelerated down the ramp.

The large numbers painted on the side and front of each car represented the driver's starting time from Brescia and in the ballot Moss had drawn 722—or twenty-two minutes past seven.

At 6.58 the first of the 3-litre, eight-cylinder, fuel injection Mercedes (driven by Fangio) left the ramp. Kling left at 7.01 and Herrmann at 7.04. As Moss and Jenkinson were pushed up on to the ramp by mechanics they both knew that their most dangerous rivals were behind them: Castellotti, with a 4.4-litre six-cylinder Ferrari, due away at 7.23, and the wily veteran and master tactician Taruffi, last man to leave Brescia at 7.28 with a 3.7-litre Ferrari.

The weather reports were favourable. It was going to be dry and hot and Moss planned to average at least 90 m.p.h., three miles an hour faster than the average of the winning car in 1954. With thirty seconds to go, the engine of the Mercedes burst into life. Moss adjusted his goggles whilst Jenkinson clutched the mechanical brain. Then No. 722 was off and the crowds lining the road on either side shrank back a little as the car drew level and swept on its way.

From Brescia the route ran eastwards towards Verona, and on the fast straights the needle of the revolution counter was steady at 7,500 revolutions in top gear, the Mercedes streaking along at nearly 170 m.p.h., overtaking slower cars, shooting over blind brows, Moss absolutely relaxed and trusting implicitly in the hand signals from his passenger.

Jenkinson knew that it would be at least ten hours before he could relax from the cryptic messages that came up in the perspex window. Ten hours of maximum concentration with absolutely no margin for error. He had another job as well—to press the horn button (which automatically flashed the headlights) as they came up behind slower competitors and passed them.

He was so busy with the route as they approached Padova that he was unaware of a dramatic turn of events until Moss pointed behind and Jenkinson saw Castellotti's Ferrari gaining on them unbelievably fast. The Italian must have been going like a dingbat, for he had left Brescia a minute later than the Mercedes and it was obvious to Moss and Jenkinson that very soon he was going to pass them.

Moss tore into Padova at 150 m.p.h., the Ferrari closing the gap rapidly, and Jenkinson suddenly realised they were in trouble. Moss was approaching a right angle bend too fast and working like a demon to slow down the car without locking the wheels and provoking a spin. Wizard that he is, he made it, and a split second before the car would have rammed the barrier of straw bales Moss released the brakes and took the corner. The left front end of the Mercedes just caught the bales, and as the car bounced off into the middle of the road, and Moss accelerated in bottom gear, the Ferrari shot past them. Castellotti's face broke into a huge grin as he looked over his shoulder.

Moss and Jenkinson had a grandstand seat for the fireworks display that followed. Castellotti was driving like a man possessed, as though the 1955 Mille Miglia was a sprint instead of a tiring and demanding ten hour marathon. With all the characteristic, fiery temperament of the Italian he slid the Ferrari through the corners, the tyres leaving vivid black marks on the road, and every now and then the Ferrari would cut through the gravel on the edge of the road, enveloping itself in a great cloud of dust.

Moss could not pass the Italian car, for it was faster on the straights, and wisely he allowed the excitable Castellotti to draw ahead. He must have wondered what would happen if Castellotti went beyond the limit on the far side of a blind corner or brow and crashed in their path. The brain was quite unable to cope with that sort of situation. So Moss eased off a little and Castellotti drew away, inside his own dust cloud.

A pensive Stirling Moss and a relaxed Denis Jenkinson wait patiently in Mercedes No. 722 for their turn on the starting ramp at Brescia. The car's number represents the time the Mercedes will leave the ramp, at twenty-two minutes past seven in the morning.
(Cyril Posthumus)

The 3-litre Mercedes-Benz SLR stands poised to accelerate down the ramp.
(LAT Photographic)

Taruffi, the last man to leave Brescia at 7.28 am, corners his 3.7 litre Ferrari between Rieti and Rome. The dense crowds are oblivious to the danger as they press forward to get a better view.
(Quadrant/Autocar)

TOP

Denis Jenkinson acknowledge
chequered flag as Moss crosse
finish line to become the first
Englishman to win the Mille M
since it was first run in 1927.
superb victory for Mercedes-Be
was one of the finest drives of
brilliant career.
(Cyril Posthumus)

LOWER

Moss and Jenkinson, faces gri
and blackened so they are ha
recognisable, are congratulate
their victory by a delighted Ru
Uhlenhaut, the Mercedes-Benz
Racing Designer. Top priority
the hand-shakes and back-sla
was a well deserved hot bath.
(Cyril Posthumus)

The Mercedes thundered southwards—across the River Po and beyond to Ferrara and Ravenna. The pace was hot and so was the Italian sun. Now, when Jenkinson was able to steal a second or two, he saw the wreckage of several cars—some of them completely written off, others well off the road and at the end of a tell-tale set of skid marks, having taken a corner too fast. The brain was certainly paying rich dividends. What was that old Army saying? 'Time spent on reconnaissance is seldom wasted.'

Ravenna, 188 miles from Brescia, was the first official control and the Mercedes slowed almost to a halt as Jenkinson held out the route-card board to be rubber stamped. Then Moss was on the move again, and to the delight of both of them there was Castellotti's Ferrari at the pits, sweating mechanics replacing its practically bald tyres.

The Mercedes swept inland to Forli, then eastwards again, following the foot of the Apennines towards Rimini and the Adriatic coast. It was about this time that Jenkinson lost his breakfast and his spectacles at something approaching 150 m.p.h. The engine fumes and heat from the gear-box had become increasingly difficult to bear, and his spectacles disappeared when he turned his head sideways with his goggles lowered. Fortunately he was carrying a spare pair, but it was days before his stomach recovered.

Moss kept his foot hard down as they tore along the straights of the coast road at 170 m.p.h., leaving the inviting blue waters of the Adriatic on their left and a trail of dusty, dirty villages in their wake, storming over blind brows and bridges, all the time Jenkinson navigating with the brain and signalling to Moss. They passed slower cars—cars that were travelling at just over 100 miles an hour but appeared almost to be on a Sunday afternoon outing as the Mercedes swooped down on them. And there were more wrecks, more disillusioned drivers who had not learned the route well enough.

But even the brain was not infallible and once Jenkinson signalled 'flat out' for a hump on a fast stretch, lined with trees, but the reconnaissance had been at fault and the hump should have been taken slower. At 170 m.p.h. the Mercedes was suddenly airborne for at least 200 feet, Moss rigid like a statue as he held the wheel perfectly still. They made a perfect four-point landing, but had Moss moved the wheel fractionally left or right it would have been the end of their race and probably of their lives.

At the Pescara Control, before turning inland, No. 722 made its first stop for fuel. In twenty-eight seconds the Mercedes mechanics fed eighteen gallons of fuel into the tank—sufficient to get the car to Rome—cleaned the thick mess of dead flies off the windscreen, checked the tyres, fed Moss and Jenkinson each with a slice of orange and a peeled banana, and gave them the news that Taruffi—behind them in fact—actually led the Mille Miglia and that they were second, only fifteen seconds in arrears. Taruffi must have been going like the wind, for Moss had averaged 118 m.p.h. from Brescia to Pescara. Of Castellotti there was no news.

Within half a minute of leaving the Pescara Control Jenkinson suddenly realised that they were in trouble again. Moss overshot the right-hand corner at Pescara station and with wheels locked went straight into the straw bales. Jenkinson vaguely wondered whether there was anything solid behind the bales and then the air was full of flying straw—it was as though a fox had got among the chickens in a hen-house.

Fortunately nothing solid halted the onward rush of the Mercedes and Moss brought the car to a stop on the far side of the bales. Calmly he selected bottom gear, turned to the right and drove along the pavement behind the bales until he found a gap where they could rejoin the road. Phew! So much drama in so few seconds! Jenkinson grinned feebly at Moss as the Mercedes accelerated.

As Moss settled down again to a tempo of flat-out driving, Jenkinson anxiously watched the temperature gauge in between giving hand signals. The Mercedes had hit the straw bales a mighty crack and it could have damaged the radiator or filled the air intake with straw. But all was well and soon the German car was in full song again, Moss working away at the wheel as the road twisted and turned to Popoli, then climbed into the mountains where he slid the Mercedes round hairpin after hairpin in awe-inspiring fashion. At L'Aquila Control Moss slowed just sufficiently to have the route-card board rubber stamped and then the Mercedes was on its way again, to Rieti and Rome.

The crowds had been bad enough at Brescia, but they were far worse on the approach to the Rome Control. The last few miles were dead straight, but the spectators on either side of the road were so thickly massed that it was almost impossible to see the road and they had certainly not left enough road width for one car to pass another. So instead of taking the Mercedes up to 150 m.p.h. plus, Moss kept the speed down to 130 m.p.h. and widened the lane between the spectators by gently weaving from side to side, horn blowing and headlights flashing.

Since leaving Brescia five hours earlier, Mercedes-Benz No. 722 had covered 537 miles at a terrific average speed of 107 m.p.h. Moss switched off the engine at the Mercedes pit and vaulted out of the cockpit to relieve himself. For sixty seconds the car was stationary and in that short space of time the rear wheels were changed, the tank refuelled and the windscreen cleaned.

Hot, tired, dirty, oily and sweaty—Moss and Jenkinson settled themselves down in the cockpit for the return leg of the course. They had good reason to feel pleased with themselves for they led Taruffi—and the Mille Miglia—by two minutes. The old saying 'He who leads at Rome never leads at Brescia' repeated itself in Jenkinson's mind as the Mercedes accelerated away from Rome Control, the harsh crackle of its exhaust as healthy as when they had left Brescia that morning.

Shortly after leaving Rome they saw the wreckage of Kling's Mercedes. In trying to avoid some foolhardy spectators the German driver had lost control, run off the road, and ended up against a tree. Kling had broken three ribs but there was no sign of him as Moss and Jenkinson passed the scene of the accident and they had no idea what had happened. For all they knew Kling might be dead.

Moss set his jaw grimly and pushed on, storming northwards towards Vetralla and Viterbo, passing car after car, using all the road and tackling every hazard in strict accordance with Jenkinson's signals. It was on this section of the course—one of the most difficult—that Jenkinson missed a signal, fortunately without disastrous consequences. Just after he had warned Moss of a very tricky right-hand bend he felt a spray of petrol playing on his neck and looked round. In that split second the Mercedes was on top of another dangerous right-hander and Moss was on his own. Fortunately he recognised the corner which was on a part of the course that he knew fairly well.

Jenkinson hardly dared look at Moss but having checked that there was no petrol leak (fuel was coming from the filler due to surge in the overfilled tank) he stole a quick glance. An irate Moss was doing three things at once: cornering, shaking his fist at Jenkinson and shouting some very rude remarks which, of course, Jenkinson could not hear.

The Mercedes swept up the Radicofani Pass, over the top and down the other side. Moss swung through a right-hand turn, then a left-hander, and suddenly the Mercedes spun, stopped almost in its own length, slid gently off the road into a ditch and brought up with a bump that dented the tail. A front brake had grabbed and pulled the car to one side, fortunately when it was going comparatively slowly.

There was no time to lose, every second was precious, with Taruffi only minutes—maybe seconds—behind them. And once again during this fantastic thousand mile drive Moss was lucky, for he was able to drive out of the ditch in first gear. He reversed a couple of times, no doubt wondering whether any other competitors were about to descend on them, and was away down the mountain road.

At Siena, that delightful old walled city, there was no information at Control as to whether they were still leading, and Moss dared not slow the average by even a fraction. The Mercedes streaked along the winding road from Siena to Florence. Undoubtedly he had never driven such a great race, and not even Fangio could have bettered Moss's performance that day if he had been sitting in Moss's seat, with the mechanical brain to help him. It was Moss's finest hour, and Jenkinson marvelled at his superb skill and the way he made it all look so easy after nearly 720 miles of flat-out driving under the pitiless Italian sun.

At over 120 m.p.h. the Mercedes streaked through the outskirts of Florence, over rough roads and tramlines, whilst excited spectators leaned far out of their windows to cheer and wave. Across the River Arno and into the Control. A momentary stop and they were away again, the forbidding Apennines between them and Bologna.

Moss covered the sixty miles over the Futa and Raticosa Passes to Bologna in sixty-one breath-taking minutes, unaware that Taruffi had retired with a broken oil pump, unaware that Fangio was stationary in Florence whose car had been hidden from their view by mechanics and officials. All that Moss knew from the slip of paper passed to Jenkinson at the Control was that they still led.

Dense crowds cheered them on as they stormed over the top of the Futa Pass, Moss slowing the Mercedes temporarily because of the danger of skidding on patches of melted tar with a layer of oil and rubber on top, left there by earlier competitors. It was here that they saw Herrmann's Mercedes—No. 704—stationary at the roadside but apparently undamaged.

Still unaware of the fate of Fangio they continued their meteoric progress. Moss drove like a man inspired, Jenkinson ever watchful as he unwound the route. Over the Raticosa Pass and clear of the Apennines, the Mercedes streaked into Bologna at over 140 m.p.h. At the Control, Moss was on the move again so quickly that Jenkinson had no time to snatch the slip of paper that would have told them their lead was now far more than two minutes.

The Mercedes was soon in full song again, devouring the long stretches of the Via Emilia at 170 m.p.h., the powerful engine note throwing out a challenge to the Italians as they tore through Modena, home of Ferrari and Maserati.

Through Reggio Emilia to Parma, the kilometre stones flashing by in fantastically quick succession, and then they were in Piacenza. Here the road doubles back towards Cremona and Mantova, and here they passed a tiny Citroen that had left Brescia while they had been asleep, also Giardini's very rapid 2-litre Maserati that had left at 6.21, one hour before Mercedes No. 722. They saluted the Italian, for he had made astonishingly good time and went on to win his class. They did not know that, of the 521 cars starting from Brescia, only 280-odd were still in the race.

The final leg at last—and the prospect of winning the Nuvolari Cup (in honour of that great Italian driver) for the car making the fastest time between Cremona and Brescia. It was a straight road for most of the way, but there were several villages as well as the final Control at Mantova, and in one village the Mercedes went into a monumental skid on melted tar which Moss controlled in his usual easy, flawless fashion. And on that final leg of eighty-five miles, from Cremona to Brescia, Moss put up a fantastic average of 123 m.p.h. At one stage the Mercedes was fully extended at 177 m.p.h.

Just outside Brescia, Jenkinson put aside the little oblong box he had grasped so tightly for almost ten hours, and a few minutes later Mercedes No. 722 crossed the finish line at 100 m.p.h., having bettered the winning average of the 1954 race by over 10 m.p.h., a fantastic, exhilarating performance.

At the official garage, when Moss and Jenkinson learned that Taruffi was out, that

Fangio—in second place—was at least half an hour behind them and that the honour of winning the Mille Miglia was theirs, the two grimy, travel-stained Englishmen clasped each other like long-lost brothers. Then Neubauer kissed Moss's blackened face and the two Englishmen braved a barrage of Latin-inspired hugging, kissing, hand-shaking and back-slapping.

Whilst Jenkinson lay in a hot bath, marvelling at the stamina and skill of Stirling Moss, the young British driver was already wondering whether to leave for Germany that night. And the tough, wiry, untirable little man did just that. At midnight, six and a half hours after arriving in Brescia, Moss drove his Mercedes-Benz saloon through the night to Stuttgart.

NUMBER OF STARTERS - 521   NUMBER OF FINISHERS - 281

Results

1.	**MOSS/JENKINSON**	MERCEDES-BENZ	**10 HRS 07 MIN 48 SEC**
			158.568 KPH (98.53 MPH)
2.	**FANGIO**	MERCEDES-BENZ	**10 HRS 39 MIN 33 SEC**
3.	**MAGLIOLI**	FERRARI	**10 HRS 52 MIN 47 SEC**
4.	**GIARDINI**	MASERATI	**11 HRS 15 MIN 32 SEC**
5.	**FITCH**	MERCEDES-BENZ	**11 HRS 29 MIN 21 SEC**
6.	**SIGHINOLFI**	FERRARI	**11 HRS 33 MIN 27 SEC**
7.	**GENDEBIEN**	MERCEDES-BENZ	**11 HRS 36 MIN 00 SEC**
8.	**SEIDEL**	PORSCHE	**12 HRS 08 MIN 17 SEC**
9.	**BELLUCCI**	MASERATI	**12 HRS 09 MIN 10 SEC**
10.	**CASELLA**	MERCEDES-BENZ	**12 HRS 11 MIN 15 SEC**

Class Winners

Sports

750 CC	**STOREZ**	PANHARD	**13 HRS 21 MIN 03 SEC**
			119.618 KPH (74.32 MPH)
1100 CC	**BOURILLOT**	OSCA	**13 HRS 01 MIN 21 SEC**
			122.634 KPH (76.20 MPH)
1500 CC	**SEIDEL**	PORSCHE	**12 HRS 08 MIN 17 SEC**
			131.570 KPH (81.75 MPH)
2000 CC	**GIARDINI**	MASERATI	**11 HRS 15 MIN 32 SEC**
			141.843 KPH (88.13 MPH)
+2000 CC	**MOSS**	MERCEDES-BENZ	**10 HRS 07 MIN 48 SEC**
			158.568 KPH (98.53 MPH)

Special Grand Touring

750 CC	**VIOLA**	FIAT	**14 HRS 32 MIN 50 SEC** **109.780 KPH (68.21 MPH)**
1300 CC	**VON FRANKENBERG**	PORSCHE	**12 HRS 58 MIN 39 SEC** **123.059 KPH (76.46 MPH)**
+1300	**FITCH**	MERCEDES-BENZ	**11 HRS 29 MIN 21 SEC** **139 KPH (86.39 MPH)**

Grand Touring

1600 CC	**GUENZIER**	PORSCHE	**12 HRS 52 MIN 46 SEC** **123.040 KPH (76.45 MPH)**
2000 CC	**D. LETO DI PRIOLO**	FIAT	**13 HRS 21 MIN 36 SEC** **119.535 KPH (74.27 MPH)**

Modified Production Touring

750 CC	**GALTIER**	RENAULT	**14 HRS 44 MIN 58 SEC** **108.275 KPH (67.27 MPH)**
1300 CC	**MANDRINI**	FIAT	**13 HRS 48 MIN 12 SEC** **115.697 KPH (71.89 MPH)**
+1300	**CASTELLI-GUIDI**	ALFA-ROMEO	**13 HRS 14 MIN 05 SEC** **120.667 KPH (74.97 MPH)**

Sub-classes

-350 CC	**CIPOLLA**	ISETTA	**20 HRS 08 MIN 09 SEC** **79.311 KPH (49.28 MPH)**
500 CC	**SEIBERT**	CITROEN	**18 HRS 24 MIN 33 SEC** **86.750 KPH (53.90 MPH)**
1000 CC	**SPILIOTAKIS**	DKW	**15 HRS 03 MIN 50 SEC** **106.015 KPH (65.87 MPH)**
1600 CC	**CAGLI-BANTI**	BORGWARD	**15 HRS 47 MIN 19 SEC** **101.148 KPH (62.85 MPH)**
+2000	**ZEDLITZ**	MERCEDES-BENZ	**15 HRS 33 MIN 13 SEC** **102.677 KPH (63.80 MPH)**
DIESEL	**LARCHER-RETTER**	MERCEDES-BENZ	**17 HRS 12 MIN 14 SEC** **94.645 KPH (58.80 MPH)**

Chapter 6

LES VINGT-QUATRE HEURES
DU MANS
11 & 12 JUNE 1955

The Circuit

LE MANS, FRANCE

Every year, in June, thousands of British motor-racing enthusiasts make the pilgrimage to Le Mans for the world famous 24-hour race. Many of them watch the race from the pits area, others walk through the famous Esses and the pinewoods to the right-hand corner at Tertre Rouge at the beginning of the Mulsanne straight. Others make their way to Mulsanne corner at the end of the famous straight which is the main road southwards from Le Mans to Tours. Others make for "Indianapolis" and the acute right-hander at Arnage on the homeward stretch. For twenty-four hours—night and day—the finest drivers and fastest sports cars battle for supremacy, with victory going to Mike Hawthorn and Ivor Bueb in 1955. Their Jaguar averaged 107.06 mph for 24 hours on the 8.38 mile road circuit and fastest lap went to Hawthorn at 122.38 mph. The fastest time over the Flying Kilometre was the 4412 cc Ferrari shared by Castellotti and Marzotto at an incredible 181.15 mph. With entries ranging from $4^1/_2$ litres to 750 cc, and speeds rising annually, the famous 4.19 mile Mulsanne Straight (with two slight kinks) presents a speed differential problem. Drivers of slower cars have to watch out for faster cars closing on them rapidly at very high speeds, particularly as they line themselves up for Mulsanne Corner at the end of the straight. Apart from this, many drivers admit to being bored at Le Mans and maintain that the most difficult problem is just keeping awake.

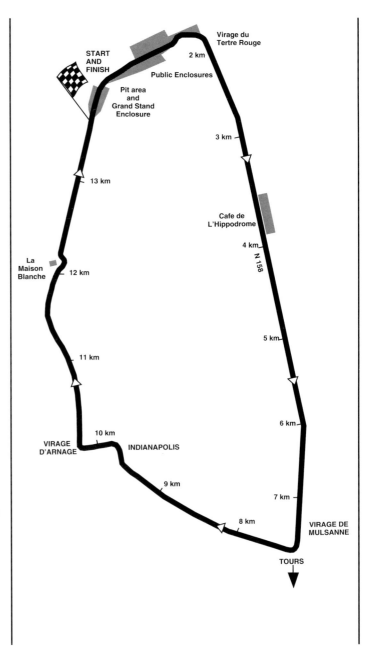

Lereck

Disaster at Le Mans

There is nothing quite like the famous Le Mans 24-Hour Race, or as it is known the world over to enthusiasts, 'Les Vingt-Quatre Heures du Mans'. Annually in June the world's greatest drivers and fastest sports cars battle from 4 p.m. Saturday until 4 p.m. Sunday on an 8.38-mile permanent racing circuit, with a surface like a billiard table, incorporating public roads to the south of Le Mans. It is a tougher test of car than of driver, for a car has to be very well prepared to cope with twenty-four hours at an average speed in the region of 100 m.p.h., whereas the drivers do get some rest, even if only a few hours. However, even though it is not particularly tough on the drivers, the Le Mans race is an extremely dangerous one because of the speed differential between the large and small cars. Most of the drivers dislike Le Mans for this reason and point out the absurdity of allowing cars which vary in their maximum speed between 100m.p.h. and 180 m.p.h. to race at the same time. With the best will in the world the driver of a slow car cannot be continually looking in his mirror. Consequently, the drivers of the really fast machinery are never quite sure whether their rapid approach—as they close on the slower car and line themselves up to pass—has been noted.

The morning of Saturday, June 11th, 1955 was just like any other pre-race Saturday morning in Le Mans. On the pavement outside Grubers' famous café every table was occupied. There were drivers, journalists, and enthusiasts eagerly discussing the long-awaited duel between Britain's Jaguars, Italy's Ferraris and Germany's Mercedes-Benz. In the Place de la Republique, opposite Grubers', the cosmopolitan array of vintage and modern cars was representative of most countries in Europe. By midday the atmosphere in the café had become almost electric, and with four hours still to go, a long line of cars and crowded, noisy buses wound slowly out towards the circuit.

This was the second year of Mercedes-Benz domination in the Grand Prix field but in sports-car racing it was a different story. At Buenos Aires in January, Ferrari had won the 1,000 Kilometre Race, whilst at Sebring in March Mike Hawthorn and Phil Walters had won the 12-Hour Race for Jaguar, and in Italy Stirling Moss had won the gruelling Mille Miglia for Mercedes-Benz. Three world championship races—one each to Ferrari, Jaguar and Mercedes-Benz. Le Mans, invariably the most publicised event of the motor-racing season and therefore the most important from the prestige point of view, was the fourth round in the series and a prize of immense value.

It promised to be a great race, for Mercedes-Benz needed the prestige of a victory at Le Mans even more than Jaguar—who had won the race in 1951 and 1953—whilst Jaguar, and in particular their No. 1 driver Mike Hawthorn, were grimly determined to humble the Germans on the circuit of the Sarthe. Ferrari for their part were intent on repeating their great victory over Jaguar of the previous year.

By 3.30 p.m. on that memorable afternoon—with a ghastly accident, the worst in the history of motor-racing, only three hours away—the field of sixty-nine cars had been formed up in echelon, in order of engine size, along the front of the pits. In No. 1 position was the $4\frac{1}{2}$-litre, 12-cylinder Lagonda to be driven by Parnell and Poore, angled so that it faced to the right and towards the famous Dunlop bridge. Along the full length of the pit balcony the spectators were four deep, the lucky ones in the front row leaning over to get a better view of the cars. On the other side of the track the crowds were jam-packed as tight as sardines in front of the grandstands.

As the hands of the clock on the Dunlop bridge approached 3.55 p.m. the drivers walked across the track and stood in a white painted circle opposite their car. By now the French police had cleared the track in front of the pits and the cars stood silent and alone—the red Ferraris and Maseratis of Italy, the silver Mercedes and Porsche of Germany, the white Cunninghams from America, the green Aston-Martins, Jaguars, Austin-Healeys, Triumphs, Bristols, Frazer-Nashes and M.Gs. from Britain, and the blue Panhards and Gordinis of France.

The flags of the competing nations fluttered gaily above the pits as the French announcer ticked off the minutes, then the seconds. With only sixty seconds to go, the thousands of people at the start were strangely quiet and only the 'flap-flap' of helicopter blades, as airborne photographers 'took a line' on the start area, disturbed the stillness.

Five seconds—four—three—two—one. Then down went the flag and there was an almost uncanny patter of feet as drivers sprinted across to their cars. Suddenly the first engine burst into life, quickly followed by others, and along the length of the pits car after car pulled away and accelerated, with a red car—Castellotti's six-cylinder, 4.4-litre Ferrari—first away.

The start of a tragic race. The three Mercedes-Benz team cars (19, 20 and 21) are pulling away from the pits whilst Lance Macklin's Austin-Healey (26) is just ahead of them. Two and a half hours later Macklin's car and Pierre Levegh's Mercedes (No. 20) were involved in a horrendous accident opposite the pits.

(Cyril Posthumus)

▶

Fangio raises the hydraulic air brake on No. 19 as his Mercedes sweeps into the Esses ahead of Hawthorn's Jaguar. When Fangio activated the air brake it was a quite extraordinary sight. Some likened it to the lid of a suitcase being lifted, others said the Mercedes looked like a pre-historic monster about to devour its prey.

(Geoffrey Goddard)

▶

Hawthorn leads Fangio at Tertre Rouge as the Jaguar and Mercedes pile on the power at the start of the four mile Mulsanne Straight where the faster cars had been reaching 170 mph in practice. The epic struggle between Hawthorn and Fangio at Le Mans was a repeat of the French G.P. at Rheims in 1953, and the enthralled crowds massed in the pits area, and at vantage points around the circuit, were priviledged to watch one of the most intense and exciting duels in the history of the sport.

(Geoffrey Goddard)

▼

▲

Two and a half hours after the start, the wreckage of Pierre Levegh's Mercedes smoulders o top of the bank that unfortunate did not protect the crowds masse behind the fencing. In a few horrific seconds Levegh's Merced hit Macklin's Austin-Healey, opp site the pits, and Levegh was kille instantly. The Austin-Healey acte as a launching ramp, the Merced became airborne and then crasl into the barrier. Parts of the car, including the engine, scythed in the crowded enclosure and more than eighty people died.

(Geoffrey Goddard)

◄ *FAR LEFT*

Four ten hours the duel betwee Jaguar and Mercedes dominated the race for lap after lap but whe Mercedes withdrew at 2 am the race was as dead as a doornail.

◄

Mike Hawthorn, smoking a cigarette, and co-driver Ivor Bue sit on the tail of Jaguar No. 6 at t end of the race. After the acciden they had to keep going, and Ivo Bueb—a newcomer to championship racing—was magnificent. He drove like a veteran, gave Hawthorn invalua support, and was a veritable towe of strength.

(Jaguar Cars Ltd)

◄ *LOWER LEFT*

Hawthorn's Jaguar in the wet o Sunday morning. It was thorough miserable as the crowds tried to shelter from the persistent drizzle was not until the race neared its end that the rain eased off, and Mike Hawthorn took the chequere flag.

(Geoffrey Goddard)

The whole field, tightly packed and cutting and thrusting for position, followed the Italian under the Dunlop bridge and swept up the rise. Within seconds the cars had dropped over the top and out of sight, down through the formidable Esses to Tertre Rouge Corner and the 4.19 mile Mulsanne Straight where the fastest cars had been reaching over 170 m.p.h. in practice.

In the Press Stand opposite the pits we had four and a half minutes to wait whilst the French announcers, at vantage points around the circuit, followed the course of that tremendous first lap in an excited, incomprehensible babble. Then far away to the right we saw the leaders—mere specks as they came through White House Corner and down the straight to the pits at over 140 m.p.h. It was a red car in the lead, and an excited murmur swelled to a roar as Castellotti's Ferrari tore through the pit area, having completed the standing lap in 4 min. 31 sec. at an average speed of nearly 112 m.p.h., a blistering pace for a standing lap.

Castellotti had the 'loud pedal' right down on the floorboards but as he lined up the Ferrari at nearly 150 m.p.h. for the right-hand curve under the Dunlop bridge the rest of the pack was not far behind. They went through so fast and so close that it was almost impossible to read the numbers—Hawthorn's Jaguar, Maglioli's Ferrari, then three more Jaguars, then Levegh's Mercedes, Salvadori's Aston-Martin, and Parnell in the big Lagonda. Fangio, after a bad start, lay fourteenth.

On the second lap Castellotti led Hawthorn by nine seconds, and the incredible Fangio was coming up like lightning. With three laps completed the order was Castellotti, Hawthorn, Maglioli and Fangio—Ferrari, Jaguar, Ferrari, Mercedes. The crowd loved it in spite of the fact that no French car was in the picture nor likely to be, for this was a three-cornered fight between Italy, Britain and Germany. Just before 5 p.m.—with ninety minutes to disaster—Fangio wrested second place from Hawthorn, only to lose it a lap later, and from this point onwards for an hour and a half one of the most closely fought duels in the history of motor-racing kept some 400,000 spectators on their toes and away from the cafés, bars, booths and side-shows that are part and parcel of 'Les Vingt Quatre Heures du Mans'.

Hawthorn and Fangio, having passed Castellotti, settled down to a duel as intense and exciting as their epic fight at Rheims in 1953 when Hawthorn won the French Grand Prix. This time however it was different, for Hawthorn was in a British car and Fangio in a German car, whereas at Rheims they had both driven Italian cars. The Le Mans duel was, in fact, between Britain and Germany—Jaguar and Mercedes—as much as between Hawthorn and Fangio, and it was no secret that Mike Hawthorn had no love for the Germans.

For lap after lap Hawthorn and Fangio fought for the lead, streaking round the eight-and-a-half-mile circuit at an average speed of over 115 m.p.h., sometimes the sleek green D-type Jaguar out in front as the cars passed the pits, sometimes the Mercedes. The German car, which was using hydraulic wind brakes similar to those used in aircraft, looked like some pre-historic monster when the flap behind Fangio's head lifted like the lid of a suitcase as he lined up the car for the curve under the Dunlop bridge.

Fangio found himself using the wind brake more and more, thus saving his ordinary brakes, for the Jaguar had disc brakes and the Mercedes did not. And Fangio knew that if he did not use his wind brake, the conventional brake linings would gradually become less efficient than the disc brakes on the Jaguar—and the British car would forge ahead.

At 6 p.m.—with thirty minutes to disaster—the Jaguar and Mercedes were sixty seconds ahead of Castellotti and the race average of 118.9 was higher than the 1954 record lap of 117.44 m.p.h. Only two seconds separated the two cars, whilst Hawthorn—on his twenty-eighth lap—had clocked 4 min. 6.6 sec., an average speed of 122.38 m.p.h., and Fangio had been timed at an incredible 168.09 m.p.h. over the measured kilometre on the Mulsanne Straight. Only five other cars of the sixty-nine that had started on that warm, summery afternoon were on the same lap as the leaders. This was high-speed precision driving of the highest order.

At 6.30 p.m., after two and a half hours of racing, it was time for pit stops to refuel and change drivers. As the Mercedes and Jaguar tore through the pit area the Jaguar pit made a signal to Hawthorn. No one can be blamed for what happened less than five minutes later when more than eighty spectators opposite the pits died suddenly in a few seconds of horror.

The leaders came into view at White House, and on the straight before the pits Hawthorn—with Fangio close behind—passed two cars. The first was the Mercedes-Benz of Levegh and the second the Austin-Healey of Macklin. Having passed Macklin, Hawthorn put out his hand and swept over to the right towards the Jaguar pit. Macklin seemed to swerve to the left, away from the Jaguar, and in that second of time Levegh in the Mercedes was suddenly faced with a gap between Macklin's car and the earth retaining barrier that was not wide enough. And on the other side of the barrier, men, women and some children were packed together tightly, watching and waiting for the excitement of the pit stops.

The Mercedes hit the Austin-Healey at over 130 m.p.h. and, in the split second before it started to spin, the British car became in effect a launching platform, projecting the Mercedes into the air and on to the top of the earth retaining barrier. At this particular point a pedestrian tunnel runs under the track, and the Mercedes hit the parapet of the tunnel with such force that the heavy engine, front suspension and wheels were propelled into the crowd. Poor Levegh was thrown head-first out of the cockpit and died instantly. As the Mercedes erupted in a sheet of flame and disintegrated, flying wreckage mowed down spectators like ninepins, whilst the remains of the chassis settled on top of the barrier and burned fiercely.

From the Press Stand we could see the smoke spiralling upwards whilst below us the first stunned groups of spectators were trying to get away from the horror and were met by others making their way towards the scene of the accident but unaware of its magnitude.

What of Fangio? Some say it was divine providence that guided him through the chaos, for he avoided the débris of Levegh's and Macklin's cars, he avoided the Austin-Healey where it had come to rest on the track, and he just touched Hawthorn's Jaguar—the merest touch that left a tiny scar of green paint on the Mercedes. Lance Macklin also had a miraculous escape, jumping out of the Austin-Healey on to the earth retaining barrier after the impact and escaping unharmed.

Hawthorn, almost hysterical, climbed out of the Jaguar but Lofty England, the team manager, ordered him back into the cockpit to do another lap before handing over to co-driver Ivor Bueb.

Wisely the stewards allowed the race to continue, for to have stopped it might have created an uncontrollable situation. Thousands of people, intent on finding out what had happened, would have converged on the pits area, and undoubtedly some of them would have swarmed on to the track before all the cars had been flagged in.

In the Jaguar team, Bueb took over from Hawthorn, whilst in the Mercedes team Moss took over from Fangio. What an assignment for Bueb, a newcomer to championship racing, to have to take over the wheel less than ten minutes after he had watched, from the Jaguar pit counter, Levegh's Mercedes disintegrate. And yet, undismayed, Bueb settled himself in the Jaguar and drove to Lofty England's orders like a veteran. Bueb was superb.

And so the race went on. But there was not a single person in the pits area, knowing about the accident, who did not pray for the night to come and go and for this tragic race to end. On other parts of the circuit tens of thousands were still unaware of what had happened.

As dusk turned to darkness the Moss/Fangio Mercedes was leading the Hawthorn/ Bueb Jaguar and the cars thundered round for lap after lap, headlights blazing, almost as fast as they had done during the daylight hours. Crowds thronged the brightly lit restaurants, coffee-bars, and beer counters in the pinewoods bordering the Esses, whilst the cars snaked through the Esses, their headlights picking out the spectators lining the wooden palings.

At midnight the Moss/Fangio Mercedes led the Hawthorn/Bueb car by two laps— some sixteen miles—but we were never to find out whether the Jaguar could get to grips with the Mercedes again, for at 2 a.m. Alfred Neubauer, the Mercedes team manager, was ordered to withdraw his two remaining cars. The directors of Daimler-Benz in Stuttgart had decided on this course of action as a way of expressing their sympathy towards the unfortunate spectators killed and injured by Levegh's Mercedes.

The German cars were lying first and third at the time of their withdrawal, with the Hawthorn/Bueb Jaguar sandwiched between them, and when Neubauer flagged in his two cars this left the Jaguar with a commanding lead of five laps over its nearest rival. With fourteen hours still to go, the race was as dead as a doornail and soon a long queue of cars crawled slowly away from the circuit towards Le Mans. There were few spectators enthusiastic enough to follow the progress of Hawthorn and Bueb through the night or of the other drivers for that matter.

In the morning, when the crowds returned to the circuit, it was drizzling with rain and the Jaguar was still in the lead, Bueb lapping at 103 m.p.h. and then handing over to Hawthorn, a maestro in the rain, who pushed up the average to 107 m.p.h. At 10 a.m. the Collins/Frère Aston-Martin had moved into second place, three laps behind the Jaguar.

Conditions could not have been more miserable. Out at the circuit, and in the cafés, hotels and *pensions* of Le Mans, motor-racing enthusiasts read the papers and many of them learned for the first time the full extent of Saturday afternoon's horror. To make matters worse, the rain seemed never-ending.

At midday there were twenty-one cars still left running of the sixty-nine that had started, and for the remaining four hours—whilst the rain poured down in torrents and the crowds stood in squelching mud—the Jaguar retained its lead. Towards the end, the rain eased off and Hawthorn took over from Bueb for the last few laps.

At 4 p.m. the Jaguar crossed the line, sixty-three miles ahead of the Collins/Frère Aston-Martin, and no one was more pleased that it was all over than Hawthorn and Bueb. As the two British drivers stood in front of the Jaguar, each carrying a victory bouquet, Hawthorn looked tired and haggard. Although he had won the Le Mans Race for his beloved Jaguars, there was no happiness in his face on that June afternoon.

Results

Place	Car No.	Drivers	Car	Distance (KMS)	Speed	Speed over Flying km
1.	6.	J. M. HAWTHORN I. BUEB	JAGUAR 3442 CC	4175.380 (2594 MILES)	172.308 KPH 107.06 MPH	281.911 KPH 175.17 MPH
2.	23.	P. J. COLLINS P. FRÈRE	ASTON-MARTIN 2922 CC	4073.020 (2531 MILES)	169.717 KPH 105.45 MPH	234.071 KPH 145.44 MPH
3.	10.	J. CLAES J. SWATERS	JAGUAR 3442 CC	3986.930 (2477 MILES)	166.022 KPH 103.16 MPH	264.124 KPH 164.118 MPH
4.	37.	H. POLENSKY R. VON FRANKENBERG	PORSCHE 1498 CC	3829.730 (2380 MILES)	159.572 KPH 99.15 MPH	225.282 KPH 139.98 MPH
5.	66.	W. SEIDEL O. GENDEBIEN	PORSCHE 1498 CC	3715.550 (2309 MILES)	154.815 KPH 96.19 MPH	219.112 KPH 136.14 MPH
6.	62.	H. GLOCKLER J. JUHAN	PORSCHE 1498 CC	3679.360 (2286 MILES)	153.320 KPH 95.26 MPH	213.904 KPH 132.91 MPH
7.	34.	P. WILSON J. C. C. MAYERS	BRISTOL 1978 CC	3654.310	152.264 KPH 94.61 MPH	242.099 KPH 150.43 MPH
8.	33.	M. J. C. KEEN J. T. K. LINE	BRISTOL 1978 CC	3641.380	151.724 KPH 94.27 MPH	227.560 KPH 141.39 MPH
9.	32.	T. H. WISDOM J. E. G. FAIRMAN	BRISTOL 1978 CC	3614.400	150.600 KPH 93.57 MPH	222.635 KPH 138.33 MPH
10.	35.	M. BECQUART R. S. STOOP	FRAZER-NASH 1976 CC	3506.160	146.090 KPH 90.77 MPH	215.569 KPH 133.94 MPH
11.	40.	G. CABIANCA R. SGORBATI	OSCA 1490 CC	3449.080	143.712 KPH 89.29 MPH	211.268 KPH 131.27 MPH
12.	41.	K. MILES J. LOCKETT	MG 1489 CC	3353.910	139.746 KPH 86.83 MPH	192.411 KPH 119.55 MPH

Place	Car No.	Drivers	Car	Distance (KMS)	Speed	Speed over Flying km
13.	49.	Z. A. DUNTOV	PORSCHE	3303.570	137.649 KPH	190.174 KPH
		A. VEUILLET	1089 CC		85.53 MPH	118.16 MPH
14.	28.	H. B. DICKSON	TRIUMPH	3263.310	135.971 KPH	222.773 KPH
		N. SANDERSON	1991 CC		84.48 MPH	138.42 MPH
15.	29.	K. RICHARDSON	TRIUMPH	3262.150	135.965 KPH	119.779 KPH
		H. L. HADLEY	1991 CC		84.48 MPH	74.42 MPH
16.	63.	L. CORNET	DB	3177.890	132.412 KPH	170.778 KPH
		MOUGIN	745 CC		82.27 MPH	106.11 MPH
17.	64.	E. LUND	MG	3156.250	131.510 KPH	186.916 KPH
		H. WAEFFLER	1489 CC		81.71 MPH	116.14 MPH
18.	65.	G. OLIVIER	PORSCHE	3155.310	131.471 KPH	182.649 KPH
		J. JESER	1098 CC		81.69 MPH	113.49 MPH
19.	68.	H. L. BROOKE	TRIUMPH	2885.640	120.235 KPH	182.003 KPH
		M. H. MORRIS-GOODALL	1991 CC		74.71 MPH	113.09 MPH
20.	59.	L. HERY	DB	2815.140	117.298 KPH	171.429 KPH
		G. TROUIS	745 CC		72.88 MPH	106.52 MPH
21.	47.	E. B. WADSWORTH	COOPER	2789.610	116.234 KPH	216.687 KPH
		J. BROWN	1097 CC		72.22 MPH	134.64 MPH

FASTEST LAP: J. M. HAWTHORN (JAGUAR) IN **4 MIN 06.6 SEC**
AT AN AVERAGE SPEED OF **196.963 KPH (122.38 MPH.)**

Chapter 7

Sensation at Syracuse

The Circuit

SYRACUSE, SICILY

70 Laps of 5.5973 KM

391.811 KM = 243.46 MILES

The Syracuse circuit is situated on the outskirts of the Sicilian port of Syracuse, well down the coast towards the south-eastern corner of the Mediterranean island of Sicily. The first Grand Prix of Syracuse was run as a Formula 1 race in 1955 when Luigi Villoresi won for Ferrari.

The fast and rather bumpy 3.4 mile road circuit—where the 1955 race average was 99.05 mph and the fastest lap 102.36 mph—is not only a tricky one but is run in an anti-clockwise direction. The circuit is in the shape of a triangle with two fairly slow second gear corners, a hairpin, and some flat-out curves. Low brick walls—a speciality of the island—border the fairly wide roads for more than three quarters of the race distance.

It is a driver's circuit where unsuspected twists appear after apparently simple bends, and the brick walls are an ever-present reminder that there is absolutely no margin for error. There is no way a driver can 'spin off' or use grass in preference to the circuit proper.

Starting Grid

C. A. S. BROOKS CONNAUGHT 2.05.4	**L. VILLORESI** MASERATI 2.04.7	**L. MUSSO** MASERATI 2.03.6

H. SCHELL MASERATI 2.08.7	**C. SHELBY** MASERATI 2.08.0

L. ROSIER MASERATI 2.10.9	**H. GOULD** MASERATI 2.09.9	**R. MANZON** GORDINI 2.09.7

R. SALVADORI MASERATI 2.12.7	**J. POLLET** GORDINI 2.12.1

J-C. VIDILLES FERRARI 2.14.2	**L. PIOTTI** MASERATI 2.13.6	**L. LESTON** CONNAUGHT 2.13.0

O. VOLONTERIO MASERATI 2.58.4	**G. SCARLATTI** FERRARI 2.30.4

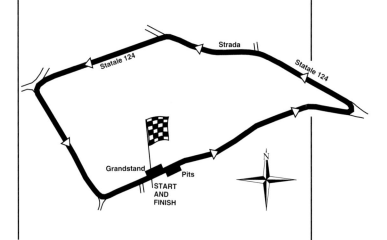

Sensation at Syracuse

*I*n October 1955, with nearly ten years of motor-racing completed since the war, enthusiasts in this country were beginning to wonder whether a British racing car would ever win a major event. For two seasons the World Championship had been dominated by Fangio and Mercedes-Benz; previously to that it had been the red cars of Italy. Admittedly, Mike Hawthorn and Stirling Moss, driving foreign cars, had won races but when was a British G.P. car driven by a Briton going to achieve success. One Sunday afternoon on the island of Sicily—with only a handful of Britons amongst a crowd of 40,000 to see it happen—twenty-three-year-old C.A.S. Brooks, and Connaught, gave us the answer.

The quiet young man—who had only a few days earlier been wearing the white coat of a dental student at Manchester Dental Hospital—was the least worried of the Connaught team. It was a Friday afternoon and the first practice session for the 1955 Syracuse Grand Prix was well under way, but there was no sign of the transporters that had left England for Sicily a week earlier with two Connaught racing cars—one for Brooks and the other for Les Leston. By using borrowed Vespas the two British drivers had been able to make a brief reconnaissance of the 3.4-mile Sicilian road circuit, but it is doubtful whether they learned very much other than how to ride a Vespa at speed.

As the 'works' Maseratis of the Italian ace drivers Musso and Villoresi lapped at an average speed of nearly one hundred miles an hour, one or two people in the pit area—and a handful of spectators in the grandstand watching the practice session—wondered vaguely about the young Connaught driver who was going to pit his skill against Musso and that master of the art Villoresi. Certainly he did not look like a racing driver—nothing hard-bitten or tough about him, just a young man enjoying himself.

Tony Brooks first went motor-racing in 1952 when he entered a second-hand Healey

Brooks

Silverstone sports car in a club meeting of the British Automobile Racing Club at Goodwood. His début was not a sensational one—he finished eighth in one race and sixth in another—but he found, in his own words, that 'motor-racing is a most enjoyable and exhilarating experience'.

At Goodwood, later in the season, Tony and his father met D. Hely, another Healey-Silverstone owner, who also raced a Le Mans replica Frazer-Nash. Would young Brooks like to try the Frazer-Nash? Tony was not slow to accept the invitation and his polished handling of the Frazer-Nash when he drove it for the first time in 1953 at Goodwood is still a talking point with members of the B.A.R.C.

Brooks raced the Frazer-Nash for the remainder of 1953 and most of 1954 to such effect that in November 1954 he was approached by John Wyer, team manager of Aston-Martin. Wyer had spotted the potential of Brooks and wanted him in his team.

Brooks passed his tests for Aston-Martin with flying colours and was soon given his first assignment. With John Riseley-Prichard he drove for Aston-Martin in the Le Mans 24-Hour Race—a frightening introduction to championship sports-car racing for this was the year of that ghastly accident opposite the pits when more than eighty spectators lost their lives. The Brooks/Riseley-Prichard Aston-Martin retired before half distance with a broken dynamo belt.

It was Riseley-Prichard who enabled Brooks to take the next step, from a sports car to a racing car. After Le Mans, Riseley-Prichard gave up motor-racing and asked Tony to try his four-year-old 2-litre Connaught. Tony took to the Connaught like a duck to water and it was his handling of the car in a number of races during the season, as well as a fine drive for Connaught at Aintree in one of their 'works' sports cars, that prompted Rodney Clark, the designer and Managing Director of Connaught, to offer Brooks a drive at Syracuse.

Although it interfered with his studies, Brooks accepted the invitation but no one, least of all Brooks, thought for one moment that the Connaught had the remotest chance of winning. Brooks knew only too well that he would be driving a modern Formula 1 racing car for the first time, on a circuit he had never seen, against several top-flight drivers and in a major continental event.

The knowledgeable enthusiasts at Syracuse were equally dubious about the chances of Connaught and showed very little interest in the British cars when they eventually arrived on the Saturday. However, they could not fail to be impressed by the enthusiasm of the Connaught mechanics who, after five days of non-stop driving across Europe, immediately prepared the cars for practice.

The second practice session commenced soon after 3 p.m. and both Musso and Villoresi were slower than on the Friday—partly because they were confident of victory and more than satisfied with their Friday practice times, and partly because a resurfaced section of the road on the last corner before the pits had tended to break up on the Friday, making the corner rather slippery. This did not seem to worry Brooks who went out in the Connaught and after a few laps started motoring in earnest. To the surprise of officials and team personnel he appeared quite at home on a fast and rather bumpy circuit that is by no means an easy one.

Situated on the outskirts of Syracuse, the 3.4-mile circuit on public roads is in the shape of a triangle, with two slowish corners, an acute hairpin, and concrete walls bordering the fairly wide road for practically the entire distance and demanding maximum concentration.

There is no real straight, but the three sides of the triangle each have fast, gentle curves. It is, in fact, what is known as a 'driver's circuit', leaving no margin for the slightest error, and the type of circuit that has always appealed to Brooks. As he himself said at the time: 'At Syracuse there is none of this business of using a foot of grass, as on an English airfield circuit, then bobbing back'.

Musso's best lap on Friday, in his 'works' Maserati, had been 2 min. 5 sec. and Brooks was very soon within striking distance of this time. He got down to 2 min. 8 sec., then 2 min. 7 sec., and finally 2 min. 6 sec., driving in such a relaxed yet forceful manner that the spectators had no idea he had put up such a fast time until the loud-speakers crackled: 'Brooks, No. 22—fastest lap of the session.'

There was consternation in the Maserati pit, jubilation in the Connaught pit, and incredulous disbelief on the faces of the bystanders. The Maserati engines burst into life and away went Musso and Villoresi, both trying all they knew to better their Friday times just in case the young Englishman managed to get the green car round in less than 2 min. 5 sec. Musso, making a maximum effort, got down to 2 min. 3.6 sec., an average speed of 99.36 m.p.h., whilst Villoresi clocked 2 min. 4.7 sec. Brooks—when he went out again—was only a second slower. The Sicilians were impressed but scoffed at the suggestion that a British car could keep going for seventy laps, about 243 miles.

The day of the race, Sunday October 23rd, was perfect and crowds filled the grandstands opposite the pits as the cars were pushed out on to the grid. As Musso had recorded the best time of the two practice sessions, it was he who occupied pole position on the front row, with Villoresi next to him. Brooks, in the green Connaught, occupied the third position on the front row, a most encouraging sight.

Brooks, Leston and the rest of the Connaught team were under no illusions about the opposition. Although it did not include the all-conquering Mercedes-Benz team—for this was not an event counting towards the World Championship of Drivers—it was a very tough nut indeed to crack. There were five 'works' Maseratis, two of which were the very latest type for Musso and Villoresi, as well as two Ferraris and two French Gordinis: a formidable array.

With the engines running and the starting area clear of mechanics and officials, the starter raised his flag. Down it slashed and, almost as one, the two Maseratis streaked into the lead, showing a clean pair of heels to the Connaught. This was to be expected for there had been no time for Brooks to practise a racing start with the Connaught.

The seconds ticked by—sixty, ninety, one hundred, one hundred and twenty—and then the leaders hurtled into view. Three red cars, then two green cars, swept by the pits in a blare of sound. Musso led, followed by Villoresi, then Harry Schell, then Brooks and Leston. This was the order for three laps and then to the delight of the Connaught pit staff Brooks passed Schell and went after Villoresi. Relentlessly, second by second, the young Englishman closed the gap until he was right on the tail of Villoresi's car, then level, then away and out in front. The Italian veteran was naturally and understandably shaken. With ten laps of the race completed the order was Musso, Brooks, Villoresi and Schell. Poor Leston had spun on the fifth lap and dropped right back.

Unperturbed, Brooks closed on Musso, passed him and led the astonished Italian past the pits. Musso fought back and the red car was out in front on the next lap—but not for long. The young Englishman was driving like a veteran, and next time round it was the Connaught again. Musso tried every trick of the trade to regain the lead and practically rode astride the tail of the Connaught. Three times the lap record was raised to more than 100 m.p.h.—twice by Musso and once by Brooks.

For a while it was real cut-and-thrust motor-racing. Musso found that by delaying his braking as the two cars approached the hairpin he was able to pass the Connaught as they entered the hairpin. However, on the exit from the hairpin, Brooks turned the tables by out-accelerating the Italian car. Brooks in any case knew that the disc brakes on his Connaught would last longer than the conventional drum brakes fitted to Musso's car.

It was plain to the Italian spectators—painfully plain—that Brooks was almost playing with Musso. He was keeping the Connaught well within its limits and driving in a relaxed, easy fashion whilst Musso was having to work like a Trojan to stay with the British car. Brooks was easily able to hold the Maserati on the fastest section of the circuit, where both cars were travelling at 150 m.p.h., and this really shook Musso.

Eventually, Brooks drew away and by half distance the Connaught had widened the gap to forty seconds and Musso could do nothing about it. On his fifty-fifth lap, with fifteen still to go, Brooks turned in a shattering time of 2 min. 00.2 sec., an average speed of 102.36 m.p.h. and a new Syracuse circuit record. It suddenly dawned on the handful of British spectators, and the jubilant mechanics in the Connaught pit, that if the green car could keep going it would be the first British victory in a major Grand Prix since 1924 when Segrave's 2-litre, supercharged Sunbeam won the San Sebastian Grand Prix in Spain.

Sir Henry Segrave, with his mechanic Dutoit, after winning the San Sebastian G.P. in 1924 with his 2-litre supercharged Sunbeam. The Brooks victory was the first in a major Grand Prix since San Sebastian.

(Cyril Posthumus)

TOP RIGHT

At Syracuse, Maserati were confident that their cars were a match for the British Connaught. However, by lap 15 Brooks was in the lead and by lap 22 he had dealt with Musso. He then lapped the rest of the field, including Scarlatti's Ferrari (No. 2).

C.A.S. Brooks had never driven a Formula 1 car prior to Syracuse. Three weeks earlier he was driving Riseley-Prichard's 2-litre Connaught at Castle Combe.

75

Tony Brooks wins the Syracu[se]
G.P. in failing light and at re[cord]
speed, having broken the lap
record twice. Fewer than twe[nty]
British enthusiasts were there [to]
see a British driver with a Br[itish]
car take the chequered flag i[n a]
major Grand Prix for the firs[t]
time in thirty-one years. It wa[s a]
great day for Britain.

(Cyril Posthumus)

◄ FAR LEFT
C.A.S. Brooks, with Rodney C[larke,]
the Managing Director of
Connaught by his side, receiv[ing]
the Ferodo Gold Trophy for th[e]
most outstanding British
contribution to the sport of m[otor]
racing in 1955.

Connaught No. 22, victorious [at]
Syracuse, being off-loaded fro[m]
its transporter for the Ferodo
presentation at London's
Dorchester Hotel.

Tensely the pit staff ticked off the remaining laps on the lap chart, slowing Brooks when it became apparent that Musso could not close the gap. When the Italian pulled out all the stops and got to within thirty-two seconds of the Connaught, the Englishman's reply was to open up the gap again to nearly a mile, and Musso finally crossed the finish line 50.5 seconds after Brooks had taken the chequered flag.

For nearly two and a half hours the green Connaught, powered by its Alta engine, a twin-cam four designed and produced by Geoffrey Taylor, had streaked round the Syracuse circuit at an average speed of 99.05 m.p.h., nearly four miles an hour faster than the previous race average. The fastest lap by Brooks was three miles an hour quicker than the old record.

Villoresi came in third—six miles behind Brooks. As the Sicilian crowd swarmed over the track, Connaught No. 22 was pushed away so that on the invitation of representatives of the Federation Internationale Automobile, the governing body of motor sport, the incredulous Maserati team manager could have the engine of the Connaught stripped down and its capacity checked. For Mike Oliver, Connaught's engine development expert and team manager, and the jubilant Connaught mechanics, it was a brilliant and well deserved British victory.

One of the first to congratulate the quietly spoken, unassuming youngster—who was persuaded with some difficulty to attend the prize-giving—was Musso, genuinely impressed by the way Brooks had outdriven him.

And what of Brooks? Never one to seek publicity either then or in later years he quietly edged away so that he could change out of his overalls and not be recognised. And on the flight back to London, the first British driver in the history of the sport to win a ranking Grand Prix in a car designed, developed and built in this country (unlike Segrave's Sunbeam which won the 1923 French G.P. and the 1924 San Sebastian G.P.) became a dental student again, quietly studying his text books.

Results
70 Laps

1.	**C.A.S. BROOKS**	CONNAUGHT	**2 HR 24 MIN 55.7 SEC**
			159.405 KPH (99.05 MPH)
2.	**L. MUSSO**	MASERATI	**2 HR 25 MIN 46.2 SEC**
3.	**L. VILLORESI**	MASERATI	**68 LAPS**
4.	**H. GOULD**	MASERATI	**68 LAPS**
5.	**H. SCHELL**	MASERATI	**68 LAPS**
6.	**C. SHELBY**	MASERATI	**66 LAPS**

FASTEST LAP: **C.A.S. BROOKS** (CONNAUGHT) ON LAP 55

2 MIN 00.2 SEC AT **164.73 KPH (102.36 MPH)**

NOT CLASSIFIED:

L. PIOTTI	MASERATI	**62 LAPS**
G. SCARLATTI	FERRARI	**62 LAPS**
L. LESTON	CONNAUGHT	**62 LAPS**

Retirements

J. POLLET	GORDINI	**LAP 9 - Rear axle**
R. SALVADORI	MASERATI	**LAP 15 - Fuel tank**
L. ROSIER	MASERATI	**LAP 17 - Drag link**
O. VOLONTERIO	MASERATI	**LAP 17 - Transmission**
R. MANZON	GORDINI	**LAP 22 - Oil leak**
J-C. VIDILLES	FERRARI	**LAP 24 - Gearbox**

Chapter 8

The Circuit

MONZA

50 Laps of 10.042 KM

502.100 KM = 311.98 MILES

Twelve miles north of Milan, in a parkland setting, Monza has three circuits in one; the road circuit, a concrete high speed track with steeply banked turns at each end of the straights, and a special Formula Junior circuit.

The road circuit is normally used for the Italian Grand Prix but in 1955 and 1956 it was run on a course that combines the high-speed track and the road circuit.

The banked track, with its North and South high-speed curves was extremely unpopular with drivers, team managers and constructors. The track was very bumpy, tyre wear was a major problem, and it was not only the drivers who were having a hard time. The cars were taking a terrific hammering as well.

It was fast—frighteningly fast—and there was the ever-present danger of going too fast on the banking, and centrifugal force pushing the car upwards, outwards and over the top.

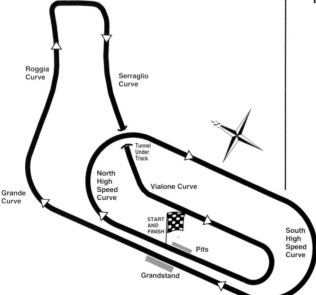

Starting Grid

L. MUSSO	**E. CASTELLOTTI**	**J. M. FANGIO**
LANCIA-FERRARI	LANCIA-FERRARI	LANCIA-FERRARI
2.43.7	2.43.4	2.42.6
S. MOSS	**J. BEHRA**	**P. TARUFFI**
MASERATI	MASERATI	VANWALL
2.45.9	2.45.6	2.45.4
A. DE PORTAGO	**L. VILLORESI**	**P. COLLINS**
LANCIA-FERRARI	MASERATI	LANCIA-FERRARI
2.47.8	2.47.7	2.46.0
U. MAGLIOLI	**M. TRINTIGNANT**	**H. SCHELL**
MASERATI	VANWALL	VANWALL
2.52.7	2.51.6	2.50.1
J. FAIRMAN	**L. PIOTTI**	**R. SALVADORI**
CONNAUGHT	MASERATI	MASERATI
2.59.2	2.58.4	2.54.6
E. DE GRAFFENRIED	**F. GODIA**	**G. GERINI**
MASERATI	MASERATI	MASERATI
3.03.3	3.02.9	3.02.6
B. HALFORD	**H. DA SILVA RAMOS**	**L. LESTON**
MASERATI	GORDINI	CONNAUGHT
3.05.0	3.04.8	3.04.3
A. SIMON	**R. FLOCKHART**	**R. MANZON**
GORDINI	CONNAUGHT	GORDINI
3.13.3	3.08.1	3.06.6

NON - STARTER
W. VON TRIPS
LANCIA-FERRARI

Battle of the Champions

*T*he Italian Grand Prix, held on the Monza Autodrome circuit twelve miles north of Milan, is invariably one of the most exciting races of the year. Often during the post-war years it has been the final world championship event of the season, and an open invitation to manufacturers and drivers alike to have one last 'win or bust' fling before the season ends— particularly those drivers who are out of the running for the World Championship. They have nothing to lose but everything to gain, for victory in the Italian classic has always carried tremendous prestige value with the Italians. The spectators expect fireworks and they get them— fireworks like the race-long, four-car battle in 1953 which Fangio won after a multiple crash on the last corner of the last lap ... fireworks like the tremendous duel in 1954 between Moss's Maserati, Fangio's Mercedes-Benz and Ascari's Ferrari. The pace in the 1954 race was an engine-wrecking one and the way in which Moss kept his engine in one piece whilst Gonzalez, Villoresi and Ascari—in that order—all retired was a fine example of Moss's restraint in the thick of the fray.

Eighty thousand spectators went wild with excitement when Moss, in his privately entered 250F Maserati, passed Fangio's Mercedes into first place and then proceeded to build up a clear lead of twenty seconds. What a victory it would have been if Moss, in an Italian car, could have beaten the Mercedes but it was not to be.

Twelve laps from the end the Maserati started losing oil rapidly and Moss came into the pits. Three gallons of oil was syringed into the oil tank in a few seconds, but as the Maserati accelerated away, the pit staff saw that most of the oil had already leaked on to the track. On the South Curve the engine seized solid, and as the car started to free-wheel, Moss clambered out of the cockpit and pushed the heavy Maserati half a mile to the finish line, encouraged by the applause of the sympathetic crowds.

Moss was the first to congratulate Fangio when the World Champion—looking very much the worse for wear after the gruelling race—had completed his lap of honour. Fangio turned to the Englishman. 'It is for me to congratulate you,' he said. 'You are the moral victor.'

Drama—always drama—at Monza but still not enough drama for the fiery Italian temperament. For the 1955 race the organisers built a banked high-speed section to supplement the existing road circuit, and claimed that the bankings would permit speeds of 190 m.p.h. and that the race average of 111.99 m.p.h. in 1954 would be bettered by at least 10 m.p.h.

A new, exciting formula for Grand Prix racing in Europe or a formula for disaster? That was the question; the Italian Grand Prix of 1955 would perhaps give the answer.

The new high-speed section, the result of nine months' frantic work at a cost of £500,000, was almost three miles in length and made up of two long straights, joined at each end by a banked turn. When used in conjunction with the existing road circuit it increased the length of each lap from 3.9 miles to 6.23 miles.

The prospect of seeing racing cars lap Monza at an average speed in the region of 125 m.p.h. was an intriguing one for the spectators, but what about the strain on tyres, chassis and drivers as—lap after lap—the field swooped upwards on to the bankings, round and down again.

It was a very real problem, for driving on a banked, high-speed circuit is vastly different to racing on a road circuit or an airfield like Silverstone. Briefly it is a question of going faster than the other man but not so fast that centrifugal force pushes the car upwards, outwards and over the top of the banking. Few of the drivers had ever driven on a banked circuit, for neither the Avus track near Berlin nor the Montlhery track near Paris were currently in use for major Grand Prix races.

There was another problem—quite distinct from learning how to go as fast as possible round the banking without centrifugal force whipping the car over the top— the constant problem of tyre wear. The concrete surface of the high-speed section was exceedingly rough, possibly due to hurried building, and the cars were taking a terrific hammering which not only damaged the suspension but caused rapid tyre wear as well. The problem was there for all to see, but the solution was highly complicated.

The high-speed section required track tyres with thin treads for high speed, whereas the existing road circuit required ordinary road-racing covers. It was up to the tyre manufacturers to find a compromise tyre that would stand up to 312 miles of racing at an average speed in the region of 125 m.p.h. for nearly two and a half hours.

On the Thursday afternoon, when the first practice session took place, it was obvious that Lancia had not found the answer. Farina had a terrifying experience on the banking when his Lancia-Ferrari threw a tread at 150 m.p.h. Grimly, on the very threshold of disaster, the Italian veteran wrestled with the wheel as the car spun—not once or twice but five times—hitting a barrier on the edge of the banking before coming to rest. The rear end of the car was damaged beyond repair and the Italian climbed out of the cockpit unhurt but white as a sheet and badly shaken.

On Saturday, to his consternation, Farina saw another tread start to lift—this time on a front wheel—but was able to stop without any damage being done. This was the last straw for Lancia, and all three cars,—which were to have been driven by Farina, Castellotti and Villoresi—were withdrawn. Happily, only Lancia seemed to be in real trouble with the tyres, and Mercedes-Benz, Ferrari, Maserati and Vanwall were able to get through the three practice sessions without losing a tread.

Following the withdrawal of the very fast Lancia-Ferraris, the Italian Grand Prix of 1955 became yet another high-speed demonstration by Mercedes-Benz, following their earlier convincing victories during the season, rather than a closely fought race. Fangio and the Italian driver Taruffi took first and second places for Mercedes-Benz, and it was the fourth successive win for the German cars during the 1955 season.

A Ferrari, driven by Castellotti, was third—45.5 seconds behind Taruffi—but although every single car and driver experienced a really rough ride on the new, high-speed section there were no blow-outs. In fact Fangio and Taruffi had a non-stop run, the winning average was 128.5 m.p.h., and Moss's Mercedes put up fastest lap with a staggering speed of 134.028 m.p.h.

So much for the bogey of tyres; the 1955 Italian Grand Prix was something of an anti-climax, but it would undoubtedly have been a very different story if the Lancia-Ferraris had not been withdrawn, for then we should have had a foretaste of one of the most exciting races ever run at Monza—the Italian Grand Prix of 1956. Packed with drama, incident following incident in quick succession, it was a race dictated by the stresses and strains imposed on the cars by the bankings, a race in which tyres played a major, conclusive role.

In 1956 the Italian classic was also the European Grand Prix of that year as well as being the final round in the battle for championship points. Throughout the entire season, prior to Monza, the main interest in a series of six races dominated by Italian cars had been the tussle for points between Fangio and Moss, team leaders of the rival *marques* of Ferrari and Maserati; and the fine performance of Peter Collins—playing second fiddle to Fangio in the Ferrari team as Moss had played second fiddle to Fangio with Mercedes in 1955. It was a struggle highlighted by the absence of Mercedes-Benz who had retired at the end of the 1955 season.

Fangio, winner of the Argentine, British and German Grand Prix—and with placings in the Monaco and French Grand Prix—had thirty points towards the championship. Collins, winner of the Belgian and French Grand Prix—and with placings at Monaco and in the British Grand Prix—had 22 points. Moss, winner of the Monaco Grand Prix only had 19 points, including placings, to his credit.

So far as the actual championship was concerned—and the final markings in 1956 were based on the five best performances of each driver—Collins would have to win the race and put up fastest lap to clinch the championship. Even then Collins could not win if Fangio won sufficient points in the race to improve the total of points in his five best performances.

In any case, it seemed a foregone conclusion that Fangio, the No. 1 Ferrari driver, would be given every chance of winning his third successive victory in the world championship series. And if Collins was ordered to hold back so that Fangio could win, there was no doubt he would do so. The young Kidderminster driver was as sensible and conscientious about team discipline as was Moss when he drove No. 2 to Fangio.

Moss, although he had won at Monaco and fought some tremendous duels with Fangio, was out of the running for the championship crown. Nevertheless, the final event of the season was expected to be a battle royal between Moss on a Maserati and Fangio on a Lancia-Ferrari—a final battle of the champions played out in an arena where there have been so many pitched battles, with Collins as an outside chance if Moss and Fangio failed to finish.

The 1955 race had not produced any alarming situations, apart from Farina's terrifying experience in practice, and the two Italian teams prepared for the 1956 race with their usual enthusiasm. The V.8 Lancia-Ferraris were firm favourites, for in addition to Fangio and Collins there were three top-class drivers in the team: the handsome young Italians Luigi Musso and Eugenio Castellotti, both men extremely fast drivers and hard on their cars, both men eager to show their countrymen who was the better driver, and the very promising Spanish driver, the Marquis de Portago. The young German, Wolfgang Von Trips, was team reserve.

The Maserati challenge was a weak one in comparison. Moss led the team with Behra, Maglioli and the veteran Villoresi in support—no more than two top-flight drivers to match the weight of Ferrari talent. Furthermore, the Maseratis had not proved particularly reliable during the season and Moss and Behra were using two new, untried cars.

Whilst it was true to say that the battle royal would be fought between Moss and Fangio it was impossible to overlook the painstakingly prepared British Vanwalls, driven by the Franco-American Schell, the Frenchman Trintignant, and the Italian Taruffi. Only two months previously, on another very fast circuit—Rheims—Schell had put his Vanwall amongst the Lancia-Ferraris like a cat amongst the pigeons, and for several laps harried the leaders in the French Grand Prix to the amazement of the Italians and the delight of Mr. C.A. Vandervell and British enthusiasts at Rheims.

The remainder of the field was made up of three impeccably prepared British Connaughts to be driven by Fairman, Leston and Flockhart, three French Gordinis, and a number of independent Maseratis.

The Monza Autodrome was open during the week preceding the race and Ferrari, Maserati and Vanwall tried out their cars before the first official practice session on Friday afternoon. There was a certain amount of gloom and despondency in the Vanwall camp for the British cars were just not tough enough to stand the buffeting on the banking, and Maserati were not too happy either. In contrast the Ferrari *équipe* was cock-a-hoop. The confidence of Ferrari was short-lived, however, for at the first practice session the Ferrari drivers found that the treads were lifting at high speed on the banking, although this did not prevent Fangio from recording one shattering lap in 2 min. 42.6 sec., an average speed of 134.12 m.p.h. Castellotti was not much slower at 2 min. 43.4 sec., whilst Musso managed 2 min. 43.7 sec. In the Maserati camp both Moss and Behra had the new cars but they were not as fast as the Lancia-Ferraris, and at the end of practice on Friday the cars with the Prancing Horse insignia were still unbeaten.

On Saturday the track was damp, following a fall of rain, and no one was able to get anywhere near Fangio's terrific times of the previous day. However, the Maseratis were quick and so were the Vanwalls—particularly Taruffi who got down to 2 min. 45.4 sec but must have shaken himself doing it, for he shook everyone else who saw the Vanwall bouncing about on the banking at high speed and almost uncontrollable.

The British cars, although very fast, were a real handful and the drivers had to ease off as they tore round the banking if they wanted to stay on the road. Taruffi's hair-raising lap was not the only sensation on the Saturday, for Von Trips had a miraculous escape when he ran clean off the road in the middle of the Curva Grande at 130 m.p.h. The Lancia-Ferrari was completely written-off, the front wheels parting company with the chassis, but the German was thrown out and escaped almost unhurt. The Ferrari team manager dismissed the accident as over-exuberance on the part of a young, comparatively inexperienced Grand Prix driver. It was very unwise, for had he but known it the accident was due to a broken steering arm and a grim warning of the shape of things to come in the race. The practice session ended with the three Lancia-Ferraris on the front row—Fangio, Castellotti and Musso—and Taruffi's very rapid Vanwall on the second row, alongside the Maseratis of Behra and Moss.

It seemed that the whole of Italy was swept by Grand Prix fever. Excited announcers broadcast reports from the circuit, and tens of thousands asked themselves the million-dollar questions on the Saturday night: Lancia-Ferrari or Maserati to win? Fangio or Collins for the world championship? Would Musso or Castellotti win the award for the first Italian driver to finish or would the wily veteran Taruffi upset the apple-cart?

One final question, a very important one to the Italians: if Fangio blew up his engine or retired for any other reason which of the Lancia-Ferrari drivers would have to give up his car to the World Champion—Musso, Castellotti, Collins...? Surely, reasoned the Italian enthusiasts, the simple answer was to call in De Portago, the Spaniard. No sense in upsetting Musso or Castellotti, and the Englishman Collins was in the running for the championship. No—De Portago was the obvious choice.

There were so many questions to be answered, and on the Sunday morning the crowds streamed out to the Autodrome in their thousands. It was raining, a damp persistent drizzle, but what matter? Fangio and Moss were masters in the rain; wet or fine, it would be a great race. As the morning wore on, the clouds drifted away and by three o'clock the track was almost dry.

With the incorporation of the high-speed section, the wide straight between the pits and main grandstand had been divided by small white rubber markers into two separate straights—the one nearest the main grandstand leading to Curva Grande (part of the existing road circuit) and the one nearest the pits being, in fact, part of the high-speed section and leading to the banked North Turn.

The starting grid was on the section of straight nearest the grandstand, and as the twenty-four starters were lined up in rows of three on the grid, the flags of the competing nations were paraded and the National Anthems played. As officials started to clear the grid the crowds packing the main grandstand noticed with surprise that a Vanwall was on the second row. This was really something, a green car from Britain near the front of the grid!

The two new Maseratis, next to the Vanwall, looked very low and long in comparison to the stubby Lancia-Ferraris on the front row, and the high-tailed Vanwalls. At the three-minute signal the first motors burst into life, and at two minutes every engine was in full song, deep-throated and challenging. One minute to go...forty seconds...twenty seconds. Up went the flag, the engine note rose to a crescendo—and as the flag slashed down, the field was away. Like a shell from a gun the Lancia-Ferrari of Musso shot into the lead, with Castellotti and Fangio hard on his heels.

Within seconds the leaders were sweeping through the right-hand Curva Grande, then right and right again at Lesmo, then down the back leg of the circuit (passing under the banked North Turn of the new high-speed section) and along the straight to the South Curve. Here they came into view of the main grandstand, and as they turned on to the straight section nearest the pits it was three red cars—with Castellotti and Musso fighting for the lead every inch of the way, Fangio on their tail.

Almost immediately they were passing the pits on the far side of the rubber markers—and streaking upwards on to the banked North Turn. Round they went to the right and disappeared, crossing the road circuit just as they came out of the North Turn,

Moss (No. 36) leads Fangio (No. 22), Schell (No. 18) and Collins (No. 26) up on to the banking. Cars and drivers came under tremendous pressure on parts of the rough concrete surface of the banked, high-speed section. The walls, in particular, though very fast were a real handful.
(National Motor Museum)

LOWER RIGHT
The Lancia-Ferraris of Castellotti (No. 24) and Collins (No. 26) on the banked, high-speed section. In practice, treads were lifting at high speeds in the region of 170 mph and the rough surface was just too tough for the Lancia-Ferraris. With only five laps completed in the race, the Lancia-Ferraris of Musso and Castellotti were both in the pits with their left, rear tyre treads in shreds.
(Cyril Posthumus)

Flockhart, who finished third in one of the impeccably prepared Connaughts, put up a magnificent performance, and coped admirably to the rigours of the banking. The Connaught suspension had never before been given such harsh treatment.
(Quadrant/Autocar)

TOP LEFT

Early in the race, Schell's Van
led for one glorious lap with M
and Fangio pressing hard. Sch
fought every inch of the way fo
thirty-two laps until transmiss
trouble ended his splendid dri

(Quadrant/Autocar)

When Peter Collins gave up his
Lancia-Ferrari to Fangio it wa
sporting gesture that meant Coll
was out of the running for the
World Championship.

(National Motor Museum)

The duel between Fangio (No. 2
and Moss (No. 36) ended when
Fangio retired on lap 19. Later,
lap 45 and with Fangio back, M
made a pit stop and Musso took
lead, only to crash. With Moss on
front again, Fangio put on the
pressure but Moss replied with fa
lap and took the chequered flag.

(Cyril Posthumus)

On lap 45 Moss ran out of fue
he coasted, prior to getting out a
pushing, Luigi Piotti pulled in b
Maserati behind Moss and nose
Moss's car to the pits.

(LAT Photographic)

then sweeping down on to the straight that led to the South Turn. Here they swept upwards again and to the right again, erupting into view at 170 m.p.h. as they came down off the banking with breath-taking suddenness, looking for all the world like a Wall of Death act.

Then they were level with the grandstand—on the near side of the rubber markers this time—and crossing the grid to commence their second lap. As the leaders went into the Curva Grande, the red-shirted Musso just led from Castellotti, Fangio and Collins, but behind the four Lancia-Ferraris was a Vanwall. 'Taruffi,' roared the excited crowd, but they were wrong for it was Schell, just ahead of Moss and Behra in their Maseratis and beginning a superb drive that was to become acknowledged as the greatest race ever driven by the dynamic, fun-loving Franco-American.

The pace was terrific and it was obvious to the delighted spectators—and equally apparent to the worried Ferrari team manager—that Musso and Castellotti were going at it hammer and tongs, no holds barred. Fangio and Collins, in ringside seats, had no wish to become involved in such an intense personal duel and wisely decided to drop back, a move that encouraged Schell in the Vanwall to rocket past into third place. Seconds later, Moss took Collins and moved in behind Fangio.

As calmly as they could the lap scorers marked off the laps (one...two...three...four), trying hard to concentrate when Musso and Castellotti screamed off the banking as though they were jet propelled, followed by Schell, Fangio, Moss and Collins, with less than a second spanning the four cars.

The race was still less than a quarter of an hour old, the crowd shouting encouragement to either Musso or Castellotti, the two Italians so engrossed in their personal duel that they gave little thought to tyres or anything else for that matter.

On lap 5 the race pattern changed—dramatically and devastatingly. Both the leading Lancia-Ferraris threw their left, rear tyre treads, and Musso and Castellotti limped along and pulled into the Ferrari pit, each shouting at the top of his voice for tyres. Moss, Fangio, Schell and Collins tore past the pits. In less than a minute the two Italians were back in the race—a race that was being run at such a tremendous pace that they now found themselves lying thirteenth and fifteenth.

On the next lap tyre trouble hit Ferrari again. This time it was De Portago who lost his left-hand rear tyre tread and found himself in the throes of a 160 m.p.h. skid on the banking. His heart was in his mouth, his stomach sick whilst he grappled desperately to control the Lancia-Ferrari as it slid wildly down the banking, the ruined cover wrapped round the wheel.

At last the nightmare was over and de Portago drove slowly to the pits where it was found that the suspension of the car had been damaged beyond repair, and it was retired.

The high speeds round the banking were imposing centrifugal loadings so powerful that the cars were under tremendous stresses and strains each time they swooped upwards and round the banking. This, and the roughness of the concrete track, was proving too tough for the tyres fitted to the Lancia-Ferraris.

The fight out in front was just as intense as when the two Italians had been scrapping so fiercely. Now it was Moss, Schell, Fangio and Collins—Moss and Schell swopping places the whole time, keeping the crowd on its feet with never a thought of sitting down to relax. Who—if they enjoyed motor-racing—could even think of sitting down with this battle going on?

The green Vanwall rocketed past Moss on the straight in front of the pits but Moss slammed into the lead again on the banking where Schell was having to ease off for fear of becoming airborne. The Vanwall was obviously tremendously fast and going magnificently, Schell driving like a world champion and delighting the crowd with his fighting spirit. Fangio and Collins, about half a second behind the Moss/Schell duel, were casting anxious glances at their rear tyres.

Further down the field Musso and Castellotti were going like scalded cats, fighting their way back to the front. And for the second time that afternoon Castellotti kept an appointment with fear. Coming off the very edge of the banking on the ninth lap, and down on to the straight at 170 m.p.h., Castellotti's left rear tyre burst. The Lancia-Ferrari pitched down the banking and, spinning like a top, slid between two of the rubber markers on to the straight nearest the pits only seconds before Moss, Schell, Collins and Fangio swept round the South Curve on to the straight.

As the Lancia-Ferrari came to rest on the grass verge, mangled rubber still smoking on the rim, Castellotti climbed out of the cockpit. He was shaken but unhurt, and the sympathetic crowd clapped the Italian for his fine effort as he walked to the pits. The car was retired with damaged steering.

After this alarming incident, attention switched once again to the battle for the lead. The giant scoreboard, which electrically traces the progress of the leader round the Monza circuit, was invariably wrong for it was quite incapable of keeping up with the ever-changing situation. Behind Moss, Fangio, Schell and Collins it was Behra's Maserati and Taruffi's Vanwall, but on lap 9 the British *équipe* suffered their first blow when Taruffi pulled into the pits complaining of suspension trouble. Within a few laps his Vanwall was out of the race, with an oil leak as an added problem.

On lap 11 Collins had his left rear tyre burst and had to make for the pits just as Schell grabbed the lead and held it for one whole lap, to the delight of the fairly large contingent of British enthusiasts in the grandstand and the admiration of the Italians who were openly incredulous of the Vanwall's meteoric progress.

Schell was by no means pulling away though, for Moss and Fangio were right on his tail and for the next six laps the gap between the three cars was almost negligible. At times the high-tailed Vanwall hid Moss's low-built Maserati and it seemed as though Schell's car was six-wheeled. This was real motor-racing, Monza at its most exciting, and the crowd loved every minute of it, particularly when they noticed that Musso, undaunted by Castellotti's experience, had caught up with Behra and was about to take him for fourth place.

On lap 18 Musso swept past Behra—the exhaust note of the Lancia-Ferrari crisp and healthy. Musso was far from finished; the race was not half run yet and there was still time to challenge for the lead again.

The nineteenth lap was the turning point of the race. As Moss and Schell tore past the pits, neck and neck, Fangio was nowhere to be seen. Then the World Champion appeared, limping into the Ferrari pit with his steering completely deranged—the front wheels pointing in opposite directions. At this stage of the race every one of the five Lancia-Ferraris had been in trouble—four of them with tyres and Fangio with steering.

Fangio was a victim of the same trouble that had caused Von Trips to crash and as he climbed out of the cockpit, shaking his head sadly, a new ripple of excitement swept through the crowded grandstand. Which car would Fangio take over? De Portago was out, Castellotti was out. It could only be Musso or Collins, and yet to take away the Englishman's car would deprive him of his chance of becoming world champion.

As the spectators argued amongst themselves and waited for a signal to go out from the Ferrari pit there was a sharp shower and Schell wisely dropped back a little, allowing Moss to go ahead. Moss, always a master in the rain, was quite unperturbed by the wet surface and had soon built up a ten-second lead over Schell.

The rain lasted three laps and had the effect of sorting out the race into a clear-cut pattern. At twenty-five laps—half distance—Moss led Schell by thirteen seconds, who in turn led Musso by sixteen seconds. In fourth place, nearly a minute behind Musso, was the Lancia-Ferrari of Collins. By now Fangio's car was in the race again, with a steering arm taken from De Portago's Lancia-Ferrari. Castellotti was driving, well aware that the rather makeshift arrangement was not entirely consistent with flat-out motor-racing. Tempestuous and fiery, Castellotti was nevertheless a brave man.

Three laps later, Schell called at the pits for fuel, having started the race on a half-filled tank so as to reduce the load on the suspension. He was soon on the move again but now in third place, behind Musso and with Collins on his tail. All was not well with the Vanwall, and when Collins swept by to take third place the British car slowed visibly. As the Vanwall came past the pits its race was almost run—the engine on the point of seizing up.

Soon afterwards, Schell was walking back to the pits, having abandoned the car out on the circuit. Both Taruffi and Trintignant had already retired with suspension failure so that this was the end of the Vanwall challenge. A disappointed Schell received a tremendous ovation from the crowd, and rightly so, for he had driven in magnificent fashion and fought it out on equal terms with the world's best.

Moss now led Musso by over a minute, whilst Collins lay third and Flockhart lay fourth, a lap behind the leaders. Flockhart, the 1956 Le Mans winner, had put up a really remarkable performance with the Connaught, having lapped steadily and without any trouble since the start of this tremendous race.

The Ferrari team manager was, not unnaturally, worried about tyres and Musso was called in for a quick check. As a front wheel on the Lancia-Ferrari was changed Musso sat motionless in the cockpit. Fangio, crash helmet on his head, waited to take over but to the amazement of everyone Musso engaged first gear and set off again in pursuit of Moss. If he expected applause he didn't get it for even the patriotic Italian crowd believed he should have given way to Fangio.

A few laps later, Collins came in for a new front tyre and on being asked to hand over his car to Fangio did so with a cheerful smile and not a word of complaint. It was a magnificent gesture for by giving up his car Collins gave up all chance of winning the World Championship. The crowd knew this only too well and gave Collins a tremendous ovation as Fangio gave him a quick, appreciative pat on the back and climbed into the cockpit of the Lancia-Ferrari. This unselfish act of Collins, one of many examples of the Englishman's sense of sportsmanship, will always be remembered.

Out in front Moss was going like a train, very much master of the situation and in no danger from Musso or Fangio, not even when the World Champion turned in a lap at 2 min. 46.4 sec. and almost immediately bettered it with a shattering time of 2 min. 45.9 sec., an average speed of 135 m.p.h.

By lap 45—five more to go—it looked as though Moss must win. But motor-racing is ever unpredictable and as he rounded Lesmo the Maserati ran out of fuel and the engine cut out. As Moss fumed at this bitter blow and coasted the Maserati—prior to getting out and pushing (as he had done in 1954)—the Italian driver Piotti, also in a Maserati, grasped the situation instantly and gently nosed Moss's car down the back leg to the South Curve and along the straight to the Maserati pit. In fact, Moss had signalled Piotti to give him a shove, and for the sake of the noble house of Maserati, Piotti had obliged.

There was no regulation preventing Piotti acting the good samaritan but neither was there any time to lose, for Musso was closing fast. The Maserati pit was a hive of activity as Moss's car was refuelled, but even as twenty-five litres of fuel was gushing into the tank, Musso's Lancia-Ferrari swept by into the lead and the crowd went wild with excitement.

Grimly, Moss tore after Musso, and as he accelerated away from the pits a mechanic noticed that the nearside rear tyre was almost bald. If Moss knew, it did not worry him, for on his next lap—the forty-seventh—he tore round in 2 min, 45.5 sec., an average speed of 135.407 m.p.h. and a new circuit record.

With only three laps to go it looked as though Moss would remain sandwiched between the Lancia-Ferraris of Musso in first place, and Fangio in third place. Even Moss—philosophic sportsman that he is—must have felt utterly miserable at the prospect of having victory in the Italian Grand Prix wrested from him yet again.

But Fate had another trick to play that Sunday afternoon at Monza. As Musso came round the banked South Turn—twenty-five seconds ahead of Moss and within three laps of victory—the left-hand steering arm broke and the tyre burst. With the front wheels splayed in different directions the Lancia-Ferrari careered across the full width of both straights towards the pits, Musso struggling to control the car and prevent it spinning. The Lancia-Ferrari eventually came to a stop within inches of the Ferrari pit counter, and as Musso was helped out of the cockpit, weak and very, very shaken, the young Italian burst into tears. To have his own National Grand Prix snatched from him like this was too much.

Now Moss was out in front again but the Maserati team manager was so concerned about Moss's tyres that he slowed down the Maserati and overlooked the fact that Fangio was only twenty-seconds behind Moss. And when Fangio takes up the chase it is usually all over bar the shouting.

The World Champion had pulled out all the stops and was driving on the limit. Slowly he gained on Moss who must have known that his tyres were in a highly dangerous state, and as the Lancia-Ferrari thundered on its way, the Maserati engine was sounding woolly.

As Moss crossed the line opposite the grandstand and started his fiftieth and final lap the engine of the Maserati spluttered slightly and Fangio closed the gap to little more than ten seconds. As Moss came past the pits for the last time and swept upwards on to the banking of the North Turn, Fangio had chopped off another second or two and went into the North Turn after Moss so fast that it seemed he must catch the Englishman.

For what seemed an eternity the crowds in the grandstand, and the watchers in the pits and on top of the pits, waited to see who would be first off the banked South Turn. It was Moss, sweeping down off the banking with a huge grin on his blackened face and throwing both hands jubilantly in the air as he crossed the line to become the first Englishman ever to win the Italian Grand Prix, and the first Englishman ever to win the Grand Prix of Europe.

The tension broken, the thousands who had watched this great race cheered, clapped and shouted 'Bravo', and within six seconds Fangio was given a similar ovation as he crossed the line for he had won the World Championship yet again. But it was Moss's day for he had driven a superb race for nearly two and a half hours at a fantastic average speed of nearly 130 m.p.h.—and had put up the fastest lap as well, as he did the previous year at Monza in the Italian Grand Prix. As one man the Italians cheered Moss again as he accepted the victor's bouquet and a Silver Cup.

What a day it had been for British drivers and British cars. Schell had shown that the Vanwall was now the fastest Grand Prix car of them all; Moss had once again shown the world that he had little, if anything, to learn from Fangio; and in all the excitement Ron Flockhart brought his Connaught home a splendid third, and Fairman was fifth in another Connaught. Finally, there was the sporting gesture of Peter Collins who willingly gave up his car to Fangio and with it any chance of winning the 1956 World Championship.

Results
50 Laps

1.	S. MOSS	MASERATI	2 HR 23 MIN 41.3 SEC
			208.787 KPH (129.734 MPH)
2.	P. COLLINS/J.M. FANGIO	LANCIA-FERRARI	2 HR 23 MIN 47.0 SEC
3.	R. FLOCKHART	CONNAUGHT	49 LAPS
4.	F. GODIA	MASERATI	49 LAPS
5.	J. FAIRMAN	CONNAUGHT	47 LAPS
6.	L. PIOTTI	MASERATI	47 LAPS
7.	E. DE GRAFFENRIED	MASERATI	46 LAPS
8.	J.M. FANGIO/ E. CASTELLOTTI	LANCIA-FERRARI	46 LAPS
9.	A. SIMON	GORDINI	45 LAPS
10.	G. GERINI	MASERATI	42 LAPS
11.	R. SALVADORI	MASERATI	41 LAPS

FASTEST LAP: S. MOSS (MASERATI) ON LAP 47
2 MIN 45.5 SEC AT 217.917 KPH (135.407 MPH)

Retirements

H. DA SILVA RAMOS	GORDINI	LAP 3 - Engine
A. DE PORTAGO	LANCIA-FERRARI	LAP 6 - Tyre failure
L. LESTON	CONNAUGHT	LAP 6 - Suspension
R. MANZON	GORDINI	LAP 7 - Fractured chassis
L. VILLORESI	MASERATI	LAP 7 - Valve failure
E. CASTELLOTTI	LANCIA-FERRARI	LAP 9 - Tyre failure
P. TARUFFI	VANWALL	LAP 12 - Oil leak
M. TRINTIGNANT	VANWALL	LAP 13 - Suspension
B. HALFORD	MASERATI	LAP 16 -Engine
J. BEHRA	MASERATI	LAP 23 - Ignition
H. SCHELL	VANWALL	Lap 32 - Transmission
U. MAGLIOLI/J.BEHRA	MASERATI	Lap 42 - Steering
L. MUSSO	LANCIA-FERRARI	LAP 47 - Steering arm broken

Chapter 9

The Circuit

NURBURGRING

22 Laps of 22.772 KM

500.984 KM = 311.29 MILES

The Nurburgring is a true road circuit of 14¼ miles to the lap and one of the most spectacular motor-racing circuits in the world. It lies 30 miles west of Koblenz. The 'Ring' is very nearly twice as long as the next longest circuit which is Spa in Belgium, and there are 178 corners per lap—ranging from some as slow as 40 mph (there is no true hairpin) to the series of three fast swerves just before the pits which are taken at about 140 mph.

There are often localised showers at the 'Ring' so that it can be dry on one part of the circuit and wet on another. It is not unusual for a driver to take one of the many 'blind' corners flat out and to find it rain-soaked on the exit. And yet last time round, the corner had been bone dry.

Starting Grid

P. COLLINS	J. BEHRA	J. M. HAWTHORN	J. M. FANGIO
LANCIA-FERRARI	MASERATI	LANCIA-FERRARI	MASERATI
9.34.7	9.30.5	9.28.4	9.25.6

	S. MOSS	H. SCHELL	C. A. S. BROOKS	
	VANWALL	MASERATI	VANWALL	
	9.41.2	9.39.2	9.36.1	

H. HERRMANN	M. GREGORY	S. LEWIS-EVANS	L. MUSSO
MASERATI	MASERATI	VANWALL	LANCIA-FERRARI
10.00.0	9.51.5	9.45.0	9.43.1

R. SALVADORI	G. SCARLATTI	E. BARTH
COOPER-CLIMAX	MASERATI	PORSCHE R.S.
FORMULA 2		FORMULA 2
10.06.0	10.04.9	10.02.2

J. BRABHAM	J. B. NAYLOR	B. HALFORD	U. MAGLIOLI
COOPER-CLIMAX	COOPER-CLIMAX	MASERATI	PORSCHE R.S.
FORMULA 2	FORMULA 2		FORMULA 2
10.18.8	10.15.0	10.14.5	10.08.9

F. GODIA	C. G. DE BEAUFORT	H. GOULD
MASERATI	PORSCHE R.S.	MASERATI
	FORMULA 2	
10.32.3	10.25.9	10.20.8

R. GIBSON	P. ENGLAND	A. MARSH
COOPER-CLIMAX	COOPER-CLIMAX	COOPER-CLIMAX
FORMULA 2	FORMULA 2	FORMULA 2
11.46.4	11.08.4	10.48.2

Fangio's Greatest Race

Of all the Grand Prix circuits none is more spectacular than Germany's fabulous Nurburgring, a true road circuit of fourteen and a quarter miles to the lap which winds up and down the mountainous Eifel country near the Belgian frontier and demands driving skill of the highest order. The challenge of the 'Ring' is one of infinite variety, for it has no less than 178 corners per lap—some fast, some medium, some slow—and is considerably longer than most circuits.

The Germans started work on the Nurburgring in 1922, partly to combat unemployment and partly to attract visitors to the Eifel district. It was built specifically as a race track and although no existing roads were incorporated it was decided that normal road conditions should be reproduced as closely as possible. The result was a punishing circuit, more winding and hilly than most roads—even in mountainous country—and embodying the natural hazards of a normal road in everyday use such as verges, hedges, banks, varying gradients—some of them swooping upwards and then downwards again like a switchback—and overhanging trees.

With such a multiplicity of corners, ranging from some that cannot be taken at more than forty miles an hour to the series of three fast swerves just prior to the pits which are taken at about 140 m.p.h., the 'Ring' is a circuit where superb driving skill pays off.

Drivers who put up fast lap times at the 'Ring'—and that means an average speed for the fourteen and a quarter miles of something in the region of 90 m.p.h.—are those who have taken the trouble to learn the circuit as well as is humanly possible. The majority of the 178 corners are blind and it is essential to know what lies on the other side, particularly when it rains. Then the 'Ring' is just about the most dangerous circuit of all, for the surface dressing throughout the fourteen and a quarter miles of its length is not constant—as is usually the case on the more normal type of short circuit—and there is no constant standard of slipperiness.

The overhanging trees make matters even worse for, after a fall of rain, moisture and sap continue to affect the surface under the trees, making it greasy, whereas the more open and windswept parts of the circuit are able to dry out normally. This means that, after it has rained, drivers have to be constantly on their guard, fully aware of what lies on the far side of a blind corner. If there are trees, then there will be a slippery piece of road to negotiate.

With the best will in the world no driver can learn all the answers, for there is a tendency for localised showers at the 'Ring'. The circuit is such a long one that it can be bone dry in the grandstand area but raining on the far side of the circuit, and drivers invariably find out the hard way. Travelling flat out, they suddenly round a blind corner to find a wet road on the far side—a very different proposition to the previous lap when the road was dry.

There is one particular hazard, between the half-way and three-quarter distance marks, that has to be treated with a great deal of respect. It is the famous Karrussel, a concrete, banked section that is more dangerous than it looks. The width of the banked section is little more than the width of a car and it cannot be taken at much more than 55 m.p.h. Anything faster is liable to force the car upwards and over the lip of the banking on to a flat piece of road, and without the banking to counter the centrifugal force the odds are that the driver will find himself shooting off the circuit like a projectile and through the hedge. There are always plenty of spectators watching and waiting at the Karussell!

The 'Ring' is just about the toughest Grand Prix circuit on cars and drivers, for it gives a rougher ride than any other circuit and calls for forty-five to fifty gear changes each lap. Drivers take a terrific pounding, particularly if the suspension of the car is unable to cope, and I well remember how Tony Brooks was physically sick during the last two laps of the 1957 German Grand Prix and had to be lifted out of his Vanwall after the race. There are several parts of the circuit where the cars become fully airborne, such as the hump-back bridge on the straight prior to the pits. In the early stages of a race, when the fuel tank is carrying thirty or forty gallons, the shock of landing taxes the suspension to the limit.

The 'Ring' has seen some fabulous races, particularly during the pre-war years from 1934 to 1939 when the German Mercedes-Benz and Auto-Union teams dominated Grand Prix racing. In those days crowds of up to half a million Germans turned out to see their national racing teams battle for supremacy. After the war the only occasion on which the Germans took a real interest was in 1954, the year of the return to Grand Prix racing of Mercedes-Benz. They saw Fangio lead the German team to victory, then they lost interest again for there was no race in 1955—the year of the Le Mans disaster—and Mercedes-Benz retired from Grand Prix racing after the Italian Grand Prix of September 1955.

And yet strangely enough the two greatest races ever run at the Nurburgring were won by Italian cars. In 1935 that fantastic driver Tazio Nuvolari—at the age of forty-two—humbled the Mercedes-Benz and Auto-Union teams to win the German Grand Prix for Alfa-Romeo, his finest race in a lifetime of superb victories. And in 1957 there was a fantastic battle between Fangio, driving a Maserati, and the two Lancia-Ferrari drivers—Hawthorn and Collins.

Juan Fangio, the World Champion of 1951, 1954, 1955 and 1956 was then forty-six years old and referred to affectionately as 'the old man', but his performance on that never-to-be-forgotten occasion in 1957 will live for ever in the annals of motor-racing.

In August 1957, as the racing-car transporters rumbled towards the Nurburgring, Fangio had already won the Argentine, Monaco, and Rouen races for Maserati—all world championship events—whilst Moss had given Vanwall, and Britain, a resounding victory at Aintree by winning the British Grand Prix, the fourth championship event of the season. It was the first time in thirty-three years that a British driver at the wheel of a British car had won a *Grande Epreuve*.

The German Grand Prix was the fifth championship event of 1957 and it soon became apparent that the Vanwalls—driven by Moss, Brooks and Lewis-Evans—were not going to repeat their Aintree success. The Vanwall *équipe* had never before raced at the 'Ring' and had very little data available about suspension. It was obvious that a great deal of modification to the suspension of the British cars was necessary and equally obvious that there was no time in which to carry out the work. The battle for the lead in the twenty-two-lap, 312-mile race would be fought out between the Lancia-Ferraris of Hawthorn, Collins and Musso and the Maseratis of Fangio, Behra and Schell.

The first practice session was held on the Friday and onlookers expected some improvement on the fastest lap in 1956 (by Fangio on a Lancia-Ferrari) of 9 min. 41.6 sec., for lengthy sections of the fourteen-and-a-quarter-mile circuit had been resurfaced. They were not disappointed; on a dry, sunny track Fangio tore round in his Maserati and clocked 9 min. 34 sec. Then 'the old man' went out again and to the amazement of the incredulous timekeepers turned in one sizzling lap in 9 min. 25.6 sec.—sixteen seconds faster than his 1956 record time.

The experts were impressed—who wouldn't be—but no one thought for a moment that Fangio would lap as fast in the race. This was sound reasoning for generally speaking the record lap in a race is slower than the fastest lap in practice. On this occasion the experts were to be proved wrong.

Fangio was not the only driver with the bit between his teeth, for Hawthorn was on form—very much so. There were few drivers who could match Mike Hawthorn on one of his good days and as he came past the pits it was obvious that he was making an all-out effort to better Fangio's time. But even Hawthorn could not get below 9 min. 37.8 sec.

On the Saturday, still dry and warm, Fangio went out but did not improve his time. However, Hawthorn was determined to get much closer to Fangio's 9 min. 25.6 sec., and hunched over the wheel in typical fighting pose he did so, clocking 9 min. 28.4 sec., only three seconds slower than the World Champion. When practice ended, the three fastest drivers were Fangio, Hawthorn and Behra, in that order. Nine Formula 2 cars had been invited to take part in the main event but did not qualify for championship points. E. Barth with a Porsche R.S. got on to the fourth row of the grid with a time of 10 min. 02.2 sec. which was a better time than the Maseratis of Halford, Godia, and Gould.

In the restaurant of the famous Sport Hotel, which stands alongside the starting area and has the grandstands built over it, the general consensus of opinion was that Fangio would bring off the hat-trick and win the German classic for the third time in succession, provided he could hold off the challenge that Hawthorn was almost certain to make.

Down in the paddock the mechanics worked on the cars whilst out on the circuit dozens of private car owners and motor-cyclists paid a small fee and matched their skill against the 'Ring'. This is a good time to stay in the Sport Hotel!

The race strategy of the three teams had already been decided. The Maseratis would start with petrol tanks half full so as to reduce weight and increase acceleration during the early stages of the race. It was up to the drivers to build up a commanding lead so that they could refuel at half-distance without losing the lead. The Lancia-Ferraris would run through non-stop, tanks filled at the start, and so would the Vanwalls. It was a situation full of promise, for it meant that there would be pit stops to make the race more interesting, and a maximum effort on the part of the Lancia-Ferrari drivers to prevent Fangio getting too far ahead in preparation for his pit stop.

On Sunday August 4th the crowds streamed out to the 'Ring'. The roads leading to the circuit were jammed, some of the cars turning into the grandstand area, others continuing round the circuit to park near one of the many vantage points. As at Le Mans, thousands of enthusiasts had camped out all night, many of them at the Karrussel.

From the Press Stand above the Sport Hotel and restaurant it was a colourful sight as the twenty-four cars were marshalled on the grid just before one o'clock. The starting area is part of a wide concrete plateau, with the pits and starting grid opposite the Sport Hotel, and a large, illuminated signboard to the right of the hotel which shows the

e Vanwalls of Moss, Brooks and
vis-Evans in the pits. The equipe
d never raced at the 'Ring' and
there were major problems with
spension, and very little time to
carry out modifications.

(Cyril Posthumus)

The grandstands are packed as
ngio (Maserati) and Hawthorn
ancia-Ferrari) take off from the
front row of the grid. Collins
(Lancia-Ferrari), nearest the
enclosure, comes up fast on the
inside.

(Cyril Posthumus)

Fangio (Maserati) and Collins
ncia-Ferrari) at close quarters in
e that centred around these two
d Hawthorn from start to finish.

(Cyril Posthumus)

Fangio's Greatest Race

LEFT CENTRE
*Hawthorn in the
Schwalbenschwanz, a section o
concrete banking near kilomet
post 19 that is similar to the
famous Karrussel but not so ste
cambered.*

(Quadrant/Autocar)

*The chase nears its end as Fang
closes on the Lancia-Ferraris of
Hawthorn and Collins in the pr
back-leg.*

(Cyril Posthumus) ▼

▲

*Fangio—cool, calm and collecte
after losing forty-five seconds an
the lead in an appalingly long p
stop on lap 12, then whittling do
the lead of Hawthorn and Collin
in Lancia-Ferraris until he took
them both eight laps later.*

(Geoffrey Goddard)

◄

*Fangio is all smiles as he
triumphantly takes the chequere
flag after repeatedly breaking th
lap record.*

(Cyril Posthumus)

progress of the leading car on each lap by a series of lights. As the leader passes a particular point on the circuit so another bulb lights up until the car itself comes into sight beyond the signboard, and the last lamp lights up to complete what is, in effect, an outline of the circuit.

Down on the grid, Fangio was in pole position, nearest to the starter, with Hawthorn next to him, then Behra and Collins—two Maseratis and two Lancia-Ferraris. It was a 4-3-4- grid so that only three cars occupied the second row—Moss and Brooks with Vanwalls and Schell's Maserati. Then four cars again on the third row: Herrmann and Gregory with Maseratis, next to Lewis-Evans (Vanwall) and Musso (Lancia-Ferrari).

It was an impressive and well-controlled start. With two minutes to go, the engines roared into life and the grid was cleared of mechanics, journalists and photographers. A small, extremely vulnerable group of officials stood in the centre of the track, a few feet ahead of the front row of cars. Each official held a board and as every ten seconds ticked away a board was raised and the official concerned scuttled for cover. Thirty seconds to go, twenty, ten—and then all the boards had disappeared and only the starter remained in front of the cars. He too ran to the side of the track, turned, raised the flag—and dropped it. They were off.

For a few seconds the cars were out of sight as they accelerated away to the left. Almost immediately, having turned back on their tracks in the South Turn, they came racing into view again—parallel to the grid and starting area but on the far side of the pits. Hawthorn was in the lead. Then, one by one, the cars swept into the well-banked North Turn—easily visible over the top of the pits—and swung left and out of sight.

It would be ten minutes before the leader appeared and all eyes were on the illuminated score-board. It was Hawthorn all the way on that first lap, and the Lancia-Ferrari driver was really motoring, for his standing lap was completed in 9 min. 42.5 sec., an average speed of 87.49 m.p.h. and only a little slower than Fangio's record lap in 1956. As the Lancia-Ferrari breasted the brow on to the plateau by the signboard, Hawthorn led by two seconds from his great friend and team mate Peter Collins. Then it was Fangio, one second behind Collins; then in rapid succession, Behra, Musso, Schell, and Brooks with the first Vanwall.

Off they went again on another lap under a hot sun and cloudless blue sky, Hawthorn pressing his Lancia-Ferrari to the limit and clocking 9 min. 37.9 sec., a new circuit record. But Fangio did even better, closing so rapidly on Collins during the second lap that he had smashed Hawthorn's record time before the loud-speakers announced it. Fangio's time was 9 min. 34.6 sec., and in full view of the grandstand he passed Collins in the North Curve at the commencement of the third lap.

Now the 'old man' went after Hawthorn and drew level with him on the downhill section to Adenau. Hawthorn shot a quick glance at Fangio as the Maserati went by, and soon afterwards, to Hawthorn's surprise, Collins went by as well. The electric signboard showed Fangio still in the lead at the Karrussel and suddenly they were due on the plateau again.

At the 'Ring' the appearance of a car as it breasts the rise on to the plateau is uncanny, for the sound of the engine has somehow been left behind and a silent projectile suddenly bursts into view. A split second later and the sound of the engine is there as well, rising to a defiant note as the car passes the grandstand.

This time a single car burst into view and then shattered the stillness. It was Fangio—five seconds ahead of Collins—grimly building up his lead so that he could make the vital pit stop. He tore round the 'Ring' in the most spectacular fashion, taking some corners in a hair-raising slide and clipping the verge at others. He was driving on the very top of his form and the Lancia-Ferrari drivers did not have the slightest chance of catching him.

On the fifth lap he went round in 9 min. 33 sec. and then cut it by half a second on the next lap. By now he was twenty seconds ahead of the Lancia-Ferraris, and Hawthorn had passed Collins again and was lying second. Not that it mattered to Fangio who proceeded to break the lap record yet again at 9 min 30.8 sec., tearing past the grandstand on the eighth lap, twenty-eight seconds ahead of the Lancia-Ferraris.

Behind Hawthorn and Collins the order was Behra (Maserati), Schell (Maserati), and Musso (Lancia-Ferrari). Then came the three Vanwalls, struggling along gamely, their drivers being buffeted unmercifully as they fought to hold the cars steady. Lewis-Evans had a lucky escape when an oil pump to the gear-box failed; a change-down near the bridge at Kesselschen locked the gears and the Vanwall spun wildly, just missing the bridge before it came to rest. A shaken Lewis-Evans climbed out unhurt.

With ten laps completed, and another record lap—this time in 9 min. 29.5 sec.—Fangio still led the Lancia-Ferraris by twenty-eight seconds. Next time round, the Maserati pit signalled him to come in, Fangio acknowledging with a wave of his hand. The crowds in the grandstand, and a dozen deep in front of it on the terrace, watched the preparations in the Maserati pit. So it was to be tyres as well as fuel. How long would the pit stop take? Would the 'old man' get away again before the Lancia-Ferraris came into view? The outcome of the race largely depended on the answer to these questions.

With twelve laps completed, ten still to go, Fangio came over the rise on to the plateau, keeping well to the right for the pits. This was it. Calmly he got out. The seconds ticked by as the car was refuelled and jacked up for the new rear wheels. Ten...twenty...twenty-five. Inscrutably, betraying no sign of emotion, he looked along the line of pits as the Lancia-Ferraris streaked into view. Wham went Collins...wham went Hawthorn...and still the precious seconds ticked away.

The Maserati was still stationary when first Collins and then Hawthorn came back down the other side of the pits, went into the North Turn and disappeared. Forty seconds...forty-five...fifty. One could feel the tension mounting as the crowd willed the Maserati mechanics to get a move on. Surely there had never been a pit stop as slow as this for fuel and two wheels? And then, to the obvious relief of everyone, Fangio was back in the race.

Up in the Press Stand, as Fangio accelerated away in third place, adjusting a fresh pair of goggles, a dozen stop-watches confirmed that the Maserati had been stationary for fifty-two seconds. Fangio had come in with a lead of twenty-eight seconds and lost it— and another twenty-four—as well as losing time slowing down and starting up again. At a rough estimate the 'old man' had got forty-five seconds to make up before he could even tackle Collins and Hawthorn again. And Collins was on his mettle now, having bettered Fangio's fastest lap by six-tenths of a second with a time of 9 min. 28.9 sec., an average speed of 89.6 m.p.h., which closed him right up on Hawthorn's tail.

Could Fangio catch the two Lancia-Ferraris? Surely not—it was an impossible task even for the maestro. If Hawthorn and Collins could keep going until the finish, without a pit stop for tyres, then a Lancia-Ferrari could not fail to win. At least that's what the crowd and many of the experts in the Press Stand were saying.

For three laps, with a heavy fuel load and new tyres, Fangio stayed where he was, not making much of an impression on the Lancia-Ferraris. Then the stop-watches started to tell a story so incredible that the announcers hesitated before they read the information passed to them by the timekeepers. By the sixteenth lap Fangio had reduced the gap from forty-five seconds to thirty-three and on the next lap he chopped off another seven seconds. In the Ferrari pit all was pandemonium as the signal board went out to both Hawthorn and Collins—'faster...faster'.

Try as they might, they could not go much faster, but Fangio could, and first he lowered the record to 9 min. 28.5 sec. and then by an incredible three seconds in one lap to 9 min. 25.3 sec. No one else other than Fangio could have won back those precious seconds as quickly as he did. On the 'Ring' there is scope for a driver to compensate any lack of speed in his car by sheer driving ability—and Fangio was master of the 'Ring' that day. Will-power, incredible courage and the skill of long experience proved an unbeatable combination.

The Maserati swooped down on slower cars and passed them like the wind as Fangio tore round the 'Ring', calmly and methodically making the best use of every single yard of road on every one of the 178 corners, closing relentlessly on the Lancia-Ferraris, chopping off the seconds in great slices. On the nineteenth lap he went round in 9 min. 23.4 sec., and the two Lancia-Ferraris were only 13.5 seconds in front.

Both Hawthorn and Collins, swopping positions continually in their efforts to go faster, must have known the 'old man' would get them; and he might almost have been pulling them backwards on the end of a rope for on the twentieth lap Fangio sliced off eleven seconds in fourteen miles—a fantastic achievement—and the crowd in the grandstand rose to their feet in amazement as he breasted the rise on to the plateau almost on top of Collins.

The crowd stayed on their feet as the two Lancia-Ferraris and the Maserati tore down the straight on the far side of the pits, and the Ferrari pit staff—frantically urging on their two drivers—looked as though they were all on the point of hysterical collapse.

As Collins followed Hawthorn into the North Curve, in view of the grandstand, Fangio whistled past Collins on the inside. Then they were out of sight of the grandstand—a pity—for the crowd missed the drama that filled the next thirty seconds. Collins, refusing to accept defeat, slammed past Fangio into second place again. Seconds later Fangio drew level with the Lancia-Ferrari, ran side by side with Collins for a short distance, then gradually drew away.

As Fangio tore into a bend—the Lancia-Ferrari close behind—he took to the grass for a moment and his rear wheels catapulted a stone back at the Lancia-Ferrari. Collins winced as the stone hit his goggles, smashed them and fell into his lap. As the wind tore at his eyes Collins went after the Maserati but the incident had dropped him well back.

In the grandstand the crowd had hardly sat down after the Lancia-Ferraris and Maserati had passed out of sight when the almost unbelievable announcement came that Fangio, on that last tremendous lap, had clocked 9 min. 17.4 sec., an average speed of 91.84 m.p.h. Then Fangio set about Hawthorn and there was a roar from the grandstand when the illuminated signboard showed Fangio in the lead, half way round on the twenty-first lap.

In eight and a half laps of meteoric motoring the World Champion had recovered the time lost by his pit stop, but he was not yet in the clear for Hawthorn still had plenty of fight. He knew the odds were almost impossible, but even so he put every ounce of effort and skill into that last twenty-two miles. When Fangio started his last lap the Lancia-Ferrari was only three seconds behind and—driving like a man possessed—Hawthorn only lost half a second to Fangio during the closing nine minutes plus of this memorable race.

At the finish, as Fangio crossed the line, having averaged 88.820 m.p.h. (faster than the record lap in 1956) for three and a half hours over 312 miles of the Nurburgring, Hawthorn was only 3.6 seconds behind.

Collins, handicapped by clutch failure since the fifth lap and shaken by the incident with the stone, was a magnificent third—half a minute behind Hawthorn. Three minutes later Collins was followed in by Musso's Lancia-Ferrari, making the Lancia-Ferraris second, third and fourth. Then Moss in the first Vanwall, then Behra and Schell in Maseratis. All these drivers had put up a fine performance—particularly Moss who refused to give in and was thrown about inside the cockpit of the Vanwall like a pea in a pod.

The tremendous duel between Fangio and the Lancia-Ferraris had overshadowed the rest of the race, and understandably so, for Fangio had given a demonstration of driving at the Nurburgring that was equal to Nuvolari's fantastic performance in 1935.

The 'old man' won sufficient points that day to give him an unassailable lead in the 1957 World Championship of Drivers. When Fangio drove away from the 'Ring' after the race he was already World Champion for 1957—having won the championship before in 1951, 1954, 1955 and 1956—and no one in the history of the world championship had ever done better than that.

The victory at the 'Ring' was perhaps his greatest race, and once and for all silenced those critics who at the commencement of the season had said that Fangio was on his way out—on the downgrade. It was almost as though he had purposely thrown down the gauntlet to Hawthorn and Collins so that he could show the world he was still the master and not such an 'old man'.

Results
22 Laps

1.	**J.M. FANGIO**	MASERATI	**3 HR 30 MIN 38.3 SEC**
			142.943 KPH (88.820 MPH)
2.	**J.M. HAWTHORN**	LANCIA-FERRARI	**3 HR 30 MIN 41.9 SEC**
3.	**P. COLLINS**	LANCIA-FERRARI	**3 HR 31 MIN 13.9 SEC**
4.	**L. MUSSO**	LANCIA-FERRARI	**3 HR 34 MIN 15.9 SEC**
5.	**S. MOSS**	VANWALL	**3 HR 35 MIN 15.8 SEC**
6.	**J. BEHRA**	MASERATI	**3 HR 35 MIN 16.8 SEC**
7.	**H. SCHELL**	MASERATI	**3 HR 37 MIN 25.8 SEC**
8.	**M. GREGORY**	MASERATI	**21 LAPS**
9.	**C.A.S. BROOKS**	VANWALL	**21 LAPS**
10.	**G. SCARLATTI**	MASERATI	**21 LAPS**
11.	**B. HALFORD**	MASERATI	**21 LAPS**

FASTEST LAP: **J.M. FANGIO** (MASERATI) ON LAP 20

9 MIN 17.4 SEC AT **147.300 KPH (91.527 MPH)**

Retirements

H. GOULD	MASERATI	**LAP 3 - Rear axle**
S. LEWIS-EVANS	VANWALL	**LAP 11 - Gearbox**
F. GODIA	MASERATI	**LAP 11 - Steering**
H. HERRMANN	MASERATI	**LAP 14 - Broken chassis**

Results of Formula 2 Class

1.	**E. BARTH**	PORSCHE R.S.	**21 LAPS**
2.	**J.B. NAYLOR**	COOPER-CLIMAX	**20 LAPS**
3.	**C.G. DE BEAUFORT**	PORSCHE R.S.	**20 LAPS**
4.	**A. MARSH**	COOPER-CLIMAX	**17 LAPS**

FASTEST LAP: **R. SALVADORI** (COOPER-CLIMAX) ON LAP 9

10 MIN 03.8 SEC AT **135.999 KPH (84.505 MPH)**

Formula 2 Retirements

R. GIBSON	COOPER-CLIMAX	**LAP 3 - Steering**
P. ENGLAND	COOPER-CLIMAX	**LAP 5 - Distributor**
J. BRABHAM	COOPER-CLIMAX	**LAP 7 - Transmission**
R. SALVADORI	COOPER-CLIMAX	**LAP 11 - Suspension**
U. MAGLIOLI	PORSCHE R.S.	**LAP 14 - Broken stub axle**

Chapter 10

BELGIAN GRAND PRIX
15 JUNE 1958

The Circuit

SPA-FRANCORCHAMPS
24 Laps of 14.08 KM

337.920 KM = 209.97 MILES

The Belgian Grand Prix on the very fast 8.76 mile circuit in the wooded, hilly country of the Belgian Ardennes is road racing in the grand manner. In 1958 Mike Hawthorn (Ferrari) clocked fastest lap at an incredible 132.356 mph.

It is a truly magnificent road-racing circuit but like the Nurburgring, it is a dangerously unpredictable circuit in that it sometimes rains on one part of the circuit but not on another.

The start line is just south of the village of Francorchamps and when the flag drops, the pack swoops downhill to Eau Rouge, then surges upwards and swings round to the right in a tight, sweeping curve. It is a fantastic start.

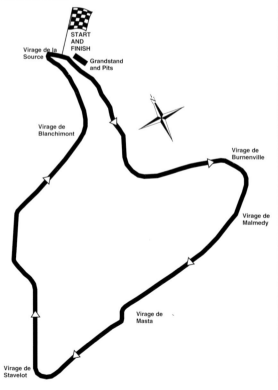

Starting Grid

S. MOSS	L. MUSSO	J. M. HAWTHORN
VANWALL	FERRARI	FERRARI
3.57.6	3.57.5	3.57.1

P. COLLINS	C. A. S. BROOKS
FERRARI	VANWALL
3.57.7	3.59.1

O. GENDEBIEN	H. SCHELL	J. BRABHAM
FERRARI	B.R.M.	COOPER-CLIMAX
3.59.3	4.04.5	4.05.1

M. GREGORY	J. BEHRA
MASERATI	B.R.M.
4.05.4	4.06.2

S. LEWIS-EVANS	C. ALLISON	R. SALVADORI
VANWALL	LOTUS-CLIMAX	COOPER-CLIMAX
4.07.2	4.07.7	4.15.6

J. BONNIER	G. HILL
MASERATI	LOTUS-CLIMAX
4.15.7	4.17.9

M. TRINTIGNANT	W. SEIDEL	F. GODIA
MASERATI	MASERATI	MASERATI
4.21.7	4.21.9	4.24.5

MISS M. DE FILIPPIS
MASERATI
4.31.0

NON - STARTER
K. KAVANAGH
MASERATI
4.55.3

Brooks

The sleepy, attractive little health-and-pleasure resort of Spa, in the Belgian Ardennes, wakes up when the Grand Prix circus comes to town. In the hotel lounges, restaurants and cafés the talk is of motor-racing rather than of the latest arrivals for a health cure. On the evening of Thursday June 12th, after the first practice session for the 1958 Belgian (and European) Grand Prix, it was of an electrifying lap time by Hawthorn, the Ferrari team leader, who had streaked round the eight-and-three-quarter-mile circuit in 4 min. 0.6 sec at an average speed of 130.2 m.p.h., and of Jean Behra's spectacular crash at 145 m.p.h. in his B.R.M. Morale was low in the B.R.M. team, for Behra had completely written off the car, but in the Ferrari team morale had not been so high for a long time in spite of the fact that British cars dominated the Grand Prix motor-racing scene. Moss had won the Argentine Grand Prix in Rob Walker's remarkable Cooper-Climax, defeating the Ferraris and Maseratis with over half a litre more under their bonnets, and then the Dutch Grand Prix on a Vanwall. In the Monaco Grand Prix in May, the Frenchman Trintignant notched up another victory for Rob Walker's Cooper, the first time that a world championship event in Europe had been won by a rear-engined car. In these three races, each one on a comparatively slow circuit, the Italian Ferraris had played second fiddle to the British cars, having followed either a Vanwall or a Maserati past the chequered flag throughout the 1957 season. In fact the once invincible Ferraris had not won a world championship Grand Prix event since August 1956.

The Belgian Grand Prix was the first occasion on which the new V.6 Ferraris had raced on an ultra-fast circuit and there was more than a fifty-fifty chance that the Italians would turn the tables on the British.

The Italians had a strong team with Collins, Musso and the Belgian driver Gendebien supporting Hawthorn, but the British opposition was formidable: Vanwalls for Moss, Brooks and Lewis-Evans; B.R.M.s for Behra and Schell; Coopers for Brabham and Salvadori. The remainder of the field was made up of six rather tired, privately entered Maseratis (there was no Maserati 'works' team in 1958) and Allison and Hill with Lotus-Climax entries.

The picturesque Spa circuit—a few miles outside the town— is part of the normal everyday road system and with the exception of the La Source hairpin just prior to the finish line is tremendously fast, with a succession of bends and swerves and one long straight that demand driving skill of the highest order. It was at Spa in 1939 that Richard Seaman, one of the greatest British drivers of all time, crashed and succumbed to his injuries; and at Spa, only a few weeks prior to the 1958 Belgian Grand Prix, that fine driver and sportsman, Archie Scott-Brown, crashed in a sports-car race very close to where Seaman had crashed, and died a few days later.

Jean Behra was more fortunate than Seaman or Scott-Brown for miraculously he was unhurt. As he went into the Esse-bend on the Masta Straight at 145 m.p.h., oil sprayed on to the rear tyres from a faulty engine breather and the B.R.M. went into a terrifying skid. Behra wrestled with the wheel and by superb handling managed to negotiate the left-hand curve, then the right-hand one before the car struck a hedge. The cowling and radiator were torn off and the B.R.M. spun to a halt. Behra, understandably shaken, eased himself out of the cockpit; skid marks nearly a quarter of a mile long scarred the road surface.

Apart from Behra's alarming experience, the Thursday evening practice session was rather quiet, with most of the drivers feeling their way round a circuit that had not been used for Grand Prix cars since 1956 but which had been modified considerably in that corners had been eased, the road re-surfaced and widened in parts, and various disconcerting bumps ironed out. Clearly the Belgian Grand Prix of 1958 was going to be won at a race average considerably in excess of the 1956 average when Peter Collins took the chequered flag with a Lancia-Ferrari at 118.43 m.p.h.

The first driver to put his foot down hard was Tony Brooks, his green Vanwall clocking 4 min. 6 sec. Hawthorn immediately reacted by equalling this time, and after a brief stop at the pits he then went out again and tore round in 4 min 0.6 sec., a speed of 130.2 m.p.h. At the end of the two-hour session no one else had bettered this time and the Vanwall drivers had obviously got to do much better if a green car was to occupy pole position on the grid.

On Friday the Vanwalls really started motoring and it was Moss who broke the four-minute barrier, streaking round in 3 min. 57.6 sec., an average speed of 132.75 m.p.h., and three seconds faster than Hawthorn. This was too quick for the Ferraris and although Musso bettered Hawthorn's time, and Collins equalled it, no one was able to get anywhere near Moss's fantastic time.

With two practice sessions completed, the final two-hour session on Saturday from 3 p.m. to 5 p.m. was the last opportunity for the Ferraris to wrest pole position from Moss. The Vanwall *équipe* was so confident that Moss's time would not be beaten that they decided not to send him out on the Saturday. In fact his Vanwall was in the garage, stripped down for its pre-race check-up, when Mike Hawthorn turned in a shattering lap of 3 min. 57.1 sec. and neatly snatched pole position from under Moss's nose.

Brooks, who had managed to get down to 3 min. 59.1 sec., was in trouble with his gearbox, whilst Lewis-Evans could do no better than 4 min. 7.2 sec. This left the door wide open for the Ferraris, and when practice ended on Saturday Musso had also bettered Moss's time and was on the front row of the grid between Hawthorn and Moss. Neither had Peter Collins been loitering; he took his Ferrari round in 3 min. 57.7 sec. and found himself on the second row, next to Brooks. With these five drivers and the Belgian, Gendebien, all having broken the four-minute barrier, it promised to be a great race.

Sunday morning in Spa, with the Grand Prix due to start at 4 p.m., was like the Brighton Road on a summer's day. The Belgian Grand Prix of 1958 had been designated the G.P. d'Europe by the Federation Internationale Automobile and cars bearing the registration plates of most European countries crawled through the main street on their way out to the circuit. It could have been the long queue into Petworth for a Goodwood meeting or the queue that winds its way slowly through the parkland beyond Buckingham to a Silverstone Grand Prix. It is the same all over the world—interesting motor cars, interesting people, all bitten by the bug of speed.

It was real shirt-sleeve weather, and out at the circuit—as the preliminary races were run off—the public enclosures gradually filled to bursting point. The flags of the nations fluttered above the pits, small groups of privileged people gathered round the cars in the paddock, and journalists of a dozen different nationalities put trial calls through to their editors.

The stage was set for the European Grand Prix—top race of the year—but there was one final dramatic touch by the organisers. The drivers were paraded slowly round the circuit in a procession of open two-seater cars, each driver sitting on the back of the seat, his name emblazoned on a king-size placard across the front of the car. This was pure Hollywood, rather like a parade of bathing beauties.

Then the nineteen cars were wheeled on to the grid and as the hands of the clock above the timekeeper's box neared 4 p.m. the drivers eased themselves into their cockpits. The two-minute signal was given and sixty seconds later the grid was a crescendo of sound as engine after engine burst into life.

Sixty seconds, especially on a sweltering hot day, is about as long as a Grand Prix car should be kept on the leash but to the amazement of the watching crowds the start was delayed. What had happened was that the two-minute signal had been given too soon and the starter was determined to drop the flag at exactly 4 p.m. for the benefit of the timekeepers.

This pantomime performance may well have cost Ferrari the race, for the engine of Collins's car started to boil like a kettle and in no time at all steam was hissing skywards. As the cars in the rear rows started to edge forward, drivers anxiously watching their temperature gauges, the area of the pit counters came alive with mechanics and onlookers waving, shouting, and urging the starter to drop the flag. At last, after what seemed an eternity, the field was away and it was Moss who swept downhill like an arrow released, Brooks on his tail. The Vanwalls swung left at the foot of the hill, seemingly clipping the stone parapet of the road bridge over L'Eau Rouge before sweeping upwards through the long, climbing right-hand bend that took them out of sight. The rest of the field, snarling at their heels, was led by Gendebien's Ferrari.

Moss really had the wind in his tail as he led the field through Malmedy Corner, through the Masta Esses where Behra had crashed, and down to Stavelot Corner. This was Moss at his best, setting a blistering pace and relentlessly increasing his lead. He took the Vanwall through Stavelot at well over 100 m.p.h. but as he changed gear from fourth to fifth, and missed fifth for a split second, the engine shrieked in protest and Moss's race was run, with less than five minutes of racing to show for it.

As Moss cruised slowly towards the pits, obviously bitterly disappointed, Brooks took the lead, closely pursued by Collins. As the cars swept down to La Source hairpin we could see that it was Brooks, Collins, Gendebien, Hawthorn, Behra, Lewis-Evans, Musso, Schell and Allison in the Lotus. As they swept over the line the incredulous timekeepers noted that the standing lap had taken only 4 min. 12 sec., an average speed of 124.28 m.p.h., and there were still twenty-three laps to go.

On the second lap, with water and oil temperature still dangerously high as a result of the start-line fiasco, Collins spearheaded the Ferrari attack on Brooks and slammed his car into the lead as Hawthorn took Gendebien for third place. In the middle of the Ferrari sandwich the implacable Brooks watched and waited.

On the third lap Brooks was in the lead again, the Ferrari so close to the Vanwall on the run downhill past the pits that the two cars appeared as one. On the next lap Collins was out in front, and the massed spectators in the pit area had their hearts in their mouths as the red and green cars, almost touching, swooped down to the bridge at L'Eau Rouge.

Unfortunately, such magnificent cut-and-thrust motor-racing was short-lived, for now Collins had to pay the unjust penalty of his engine overheating on the start line. He could feel that the engine had lost its edge, and gradually the tail of Brooks's Vanwall drew away. Collins had run his race.

On a sweltering hot day, in a
perfect wooded setting at Spa, the
Vanwalls of Moss and Brooks lead
Gendebien's Ferrari into Eau
Rouge before swooping upwards
and out of sight. Within five
minutes Moss—who was setting a
blistering pace—was out of the
race, the Vanwall's engine over-
revved. The solitary car left on the
start line, with steam hissing
skywards, is the Collins Ferrari
which overheated when the start
was delayed after the two-minute
signal had been given too soon.

(Top - National Motor Museum)
(Lower - Geoffrey Goddard)

▶
▼

▶

Hawthorn on the last lap of this
drama-filled race, having just
broken his own lap record at
132.36 mph in a desperate but
forlorn attempt to catch Brooks in
the Vanwall, goes into the hairpin
just before the finish line. As the
Ferrari crossed the line—21
seconds behind the Vanwall—the
engine blew up in a cloud of
smoke and steam.

(Geoffrey Goddard)

TOP LEFT

*The Vanwall never missed a be[at]
but on the last lap the gearbox
tightened as Brooks came out of
La Source hairpin, and the
Vanwall crawled slowly to the
finish line.*
(Geoffrey Goddard)

TOP RIGHT

*A jubilant Brooks after a faultles[s]
display of precision driving on [a]
very demanding circuit.*

◄

*Imperturbable Tony Brooks. On
his day no one could catch him*
(Geoffrey Goddard)

More drama was to follow. As Brooks increased his lead over Hawthorn—now in second place—Musso, in third place, got out of control at Stavelot. To the amazement of the onlookers, who watched horrified as the Ferrari slewed drunkenly with a burst tyre and crashed, Musso stepped unharmed from the wreckage.

Out in front, Brooks and Hawthorn saw nothing of Musso's crash, but Hawthorn noticed a Ferrari coasting into the pits and mistakenly assumed it was Musso. At this stage Hawthorn was 1.8 seconds behind Brooks and was at a loss to understand what had happened to his old friend Collins.

At Stavelot, Hawthorn saw the wrecked Ferrari—and it was a real wreck, with bits and pieces of the red car littering the road. So this was what happened to Collins. Sick in the stomach and certain in his own mind that his friend was dead, Hawthorn began to lose ground to Brooks. The Vanwall was going like a train, Brooks driving the race of his life and completely in command of the situation as he reeled off lap after lap at an average speed in the region of 130 m.p.h.

By half-distance Brooks led the European Grand Prix by thirty-seven seconds, having put up a very fast time on his fifth lap of 4 min. 0.2 sec., an average of 131.1 m.p.h., whilst Hawthorn lay second—forty-seven seconds ahead of Lewis-Evans. Was this to be the race pattern for the remaining twelve laps?

The answer was in the negative for as Hawthorn passed the pits a few laps later he saw Peter Collins standing there. The effect on Hawthorn was electrifying. Relieved, and maybe a little angry with himself for mistakenly thinking Collins had crashed, Hawthorn gritted his teeth, hunched himself over the wheel in that characteristic fighting pose of his that we all knew so well and went after Brooks.

On his seventeenth lap Hawthorn bettered Brooks' fastest lap with a sizzling time of 3 min. 59.3 sec. but he had set himself a stupendous task for, with only seven laps to go, Brooks was more than half a minute ahead of the Ferrari.

Nevertheless, Hawthorn pressed on, refusing to accept defeat and chopping three seconds off the Vanwall's lead on one lap! Out in front the imperturbable Brooks drove a classic race, well aware from his pit that Hawthorn was driving like a man possessed, but disciplined enough to drive strictly to pit orders. Brooks did not panic, and tensely the crowds around the circuit listened to the announcer ticking off the progress of the Vanwall on its final lap. Malmedy...Stavelot...Blanchimont, and then we could see the green car as it streaked into view and braked for La Source. What we could not see was Hawthorn, going like a scalded cat on his final lap and about to break his own lap record.

There was more drama to come in this tremendous Belgian Grand Prix. As the Vanwall came out of the hairpin we could see that Brooks was in trouble with his gears. Sure enough, in the cockpit of the Vanwall Brooks felt a tightening in the gearbox and as he approached the finishing line, trying desperately to find a gear, we half expected to see Hawthorn rocket into view. And then Brooks found a gear—third to be exact—and took the chequered flag after just over an hour and a half of flat-out motor-racing.

Whether or not the Vanwall could have completed another lap will never be known, but what we do know is that Hawthorn's Ferrari could not have done so. Twenty-one seconds after Brooks had entered the hairpin the meteoric Hawthorn appeared on the scene, and as the red car stormed out of the hairpin and crossed the finishing line there was a cloud of white smoke from the exhaust as the engine blew up.

In the timekeeper's box there was consternation. Hawthorn on his last desperate lap had clocked the fastest time of the day in 3 min. 58.3 sec., an average speed of 132.356 m.p.h.

We had barely recovered from this fantastic finish when Lewis-Evans appeared at the hairpin, the Vanwall limping round to take third place with a broken wishbone! What a race, and what a fine victory for Tony Brooks who took over where his team leader Moss left off, and went on to win his first victory in a world championship Grand Prix event in the face of the fiercest partisan opposition and on one of the fastest, most difficult and dangerous circuits in the world.

Results
24 Laps

1.	**C.A.S. BROOKS**	VANWALL	**1 HR 37 MIN 06.3 SEC**	
			209.090 KPH (129.922 MPH)	
2.	**J.M. HAWTHORN**	FERRARI	**1 HR 37 MIN 27.0 SEC**	
3.	**S. LEWIS-EVANS**	VANWALL	**1 HR 40 MIN 07.2 SEC**	
4.	**C. ALLISON**	LOTUS-CLIMAX	**1 HR 41 MIN 21.8 SEC**	
5.	**H. SCHELL**	B.R.M.	**23 LAPS**	
6.	**O. GENDEBIEN**	FERRARI	**23 LAPS**	
7.	**M. TRINTIGNANT**	MASERATI	**23 LAPS**	
8.	**R. SALVADORI**	COOPER-CLIMAX	**23 LAPS**	
9.	**J. BONNIER**	MASERATI	**22 LAPS**	
10.	**MISS M. DE FILIPPIS**	MASERATI	**22 LAPS**	

FASTEST LAP: **J.M. HAWTHORN** (FERRARI) ON LAP 24

3 MIN 58.3 SEC AT **213.008 KPH (132.356 MPH)**

Retirements

M. GREGORY	MASERATI	**LAP 1 - Engine**
S. MOSS	VANWALL	**LAP 1 - Engine**
W. SEIDEL	MASERATI	**LAP 4 - Rear axle**
P. COLLINS	FERRARI	**LAP 5 - Overheating**
J. BEHRA	B.R.M.	**LAP 5 - Oil pressure**
L. MUSSO	FERRARI	**LAP 6 - Tyre burst**
G. HILL	LOTUS-CLIMAX	**LAP 12 - Engine**
J. BRABHAM	COOPER-CLIMAX	**LAP 17 - Overheating**
F. GODIA	MASERATI	**LAP 21 - Engine**

Chapter 11

MOROCCAN GRAND PRIX
19 OCTOBER 1958

The Circuit

AIN DIAB, Casablanca

53 Laps of 7.618 KM

403.75 KM = 250.88 MILES

The Moroccan Grand Prix, first held in 1930 as a handicap event, was revived as a Formula 1 event in 1957. For 1958 the race was granted world championship status. With a 1958 race average of 116.461 mph and a fastest lap of 119.334 mph, Ain-Diab is a very fast circuit, just south of Casablanca and bordered on its northern side—where the grandstands and pits are located—by the Atlantic.

In spite of its fast corners or swerves—and there are more fast swerves than straight sections—the 4.7 mile road circuit unfortunately lacks the true road circuit atmosphere because it is fairly open country and rather featureless.

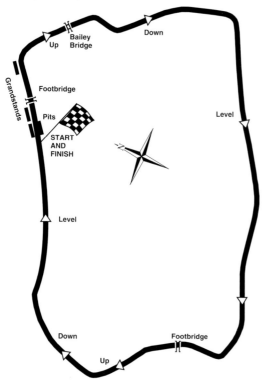

Starting Grid

S. LEWIS-EVANS	S. MOSS	J. M. HAWTHORN
VANWALL	VANWALL	FERRARI
2.23.7	2.23.2	2.23.1

P. HILL	J. BEHRA
FERRARI	B.R.M.
2.24.1	2.23.8

J. BONNIER	C.A.S. BROOKS	O. GENDEBIEN
B.R.M.	VANWALL	FERRARI
2.24.9	2.24.4	2.24.3

H. SCHELL	M. TRINTIGNANT
B.R.M.	COOPER-CLIMAX
2.26.4	2.26.0

M. GREGORY	G. HILL	J. FAIRMAN
MASERATI	LOTUS-CLIMAX	COOPER-CLIMAX
2.27.6	2.27.1	2.27.0

R. FLOCKHART	R. SALVADORI
B.R.M.	COOPER-CLIMAX
2.29.8	2.28.6

H. HERRMANN	G. GERINI	C. ALLISON
MASERATI	MASERATI	LOTUS-CLIMAX
2.35.1	2.35.1	2.33.7

W. SEIDEL	J. BRABHAM
MASERATI	COOPER-CLIMAX
2.38.2	FORMULA 2
	2.36.6

R. LACAZE	T. BRIDGER	B. Mc LAREN
COOPER-CLIMAX	COOPER-CLIMAX	COOPER-CLIMAX
FORMULA 2	FORMULA 2	FORMULA 2
2.43.1	2.42.5	2.41.7

A. GUELFI	F. PICARD
COOPER-CLIMAX	COOPER-CLIMAX
FORMULA 2	FORMULA 2
2.47.8	2.46.4

Loser Takes All

Of the many British drivers who have fought so tenaciously in the post-war years to bring motor-racing prestige to this country there are two in particular who stand out above the others. One is Stirling Crauford Moss and the other the late John Michael Hawthorn who died so tragically in a road accident in January 1959. Their achievements—Moss with Maserati, Mercedes-Benz, and Vanwall and Hawthorn with Ferrari and Jaguar—will never be forgotten.

Over four seasons, from 1954 (when Moss drove his private 250F Maserati and Hawthorn was already with Ferrari) until 1957, these two superb drivers battled for points in the annual World Championship of Drivers, neither of them able to wrest the championship from the incredible Fangio who won it every year from 1954 to 1957.

The picture was a different one in 1958 for this was a championship season dominated by British drivers who won nine out of the ten world championship races and recorded fastest lap of the day in eight of them; a season when Moss and Hawthorn fought for the world title from the Argentine and through the European series to a magnificent climax at Casablanca in October 1958.

It was a great season for British cars—a Golden Year—for they won eight of the ten championship events and Ferrari won the other two. But it was a tragic season as well for Britain lost Peter Collins and Stuart Lewis-Evans in Grand Prix racing, and Archie Scott-Brown in sports-car racing.

Moss was with Vanwall in 1958, Hawthorn with Ferrari, and when the season opened, the $2\frac{1}{2}$-litre, 4-cylinder fuel-injection Vanwall had been well and truly blooded. In July 1957 Moss had won the British Grand Prix at Aintree, after his own car had broken down and he had taken over the Vanwall of Brooks. This victory for millionaire industrialist and patriot C.A. Vandervell was of inestimable prestige value for it was the first time a British car and driver had won a *Grande Epreuve* since 1923.

To show it was no fluke the Vanwalls won two more world championship events before the season ended. Moss was victorious at Pescara and again at Monza. On the crest of the wave at last the cars in British racing green were ready to challenge the world.

The 1958 season opened as usual with the Argentine Grand Prix and although the Vanwall team did not make the long journey to the Argentine, Moss was there. With Rob Walker's astonishing Cooper-Climax he beat the Ferraris of Hawthorn and Musso, also Fangio's Maserati, and won his first championship points of the season. In the Monaco Grand Prix, Rob Walker's car again beat the Ferraris—this time in the hands of the French driver Trintignant—but all three Vanwalls retired.

In the Dutch Grand Prix Moss kept his Vanwall in front from start to finish and the Ferraris were never in the picture. On the exacting Spa circuit in the Belgian Grand Prix Brooks won for Vanwall and Hawthorn was second. Two wins for Moss, one for Brooks and one for Trintignant, but nothing yet for Hawthorn.

The French Grand Prix on the fast Rheims circuit was the last appearance in a world championship event of Juan Manuel Fangio, one of the greatest—if not the greatest—racing drivers of all time. He was forty-seven when he retired, almost twice the age of Hawthorn, Brooks, Moss and Collins.

Hawthorn led the race from start to finish and Moss was second—sandwiched between Hawthorn's Ferrari and the Ferrari driven by Von Trips. Fangio finished fourth in his Maserati which was down on power and also had gear pre-selector problems.

It was a sad day for the Italians, their first victory of 1958, for young Luigi Musso was killed when he lost control of his Ferrari at over 120 m.p.h. on the long, sweeping curve after the pits. Two weeks later at Silverstone Ferrari won the British Grand Prix. This time it was Peter Collins who took the chequered flag—whilst his great friend and team leader, Hawthorn, finished second and put up fastest lap as well.

On August 3rd, in the German Grand Prix at the Nurburgring, Hawthorn and Collins met the Vanwalls again. It was a tragic day, for soon after Brooks' Vanwall had wrested the lead from the two Ferraris—racing in close company—Collins crashed as he followed Brooks into a steeply-climbing right-hand turn. Hawthorn, only a few yards behind, saw his friend career off the road to the left, hit the bank and overturn. Collins was thrown out and in a matter of hours had succumbed to his injuries. Hawthorn, shaken and bewildered, retired soon after the crash and Brooks went on to win.

Three weeks later, in the Grand Prix of Portugal at Oporto, Hawthorn took up the challenge again, displaying that same brand of courage that had seen him through the Le Mans race of 1955 after the ghastly multiple accident. Mike Hawthorn had guts, of that there will never be any doubt, for to race again so soon after his friend's death demanded courage of the highest order.

By now, with three more races still to be run, the odds in the World Championship were slightly in favour of Hawthorn. He had gained 30 points since the commencement of the season whilst Moss had 24.

The championship marking system in 1958 awarded points in each race for all placings from first to fifth and for fastest lap. Hawthorn had scored 4 points in the Argentine (third place), 1 at Monaco (fastest lap), 2 in the Dutch G.P. (fifth place), 7 in the Belgian G.P. (second place and fastest lap), 9 in the French G.P. (first place and fastest lap), and 7 in the British G.P. (second place and fastest lap).

Moss had scored his points in only four races, not having finished in the others. The markings gave him 8 in the Argentine G.P. (first place), 9 in the Dutch G.P. (first place and fastest lap), 6 in the French G.P. (second place), and 1 in the German G.P. for fastest lap.

It was the Grand Prix of Portugal that provided high drama in the struggle between these two for the championship. Moss took the lead from Hawthorn on lap 8 and went on to win in immaculate fashion. It was Moss at his brilliant best, absolutely uncatchable and driving on top of his form, but it was Hawthorn who put up fastest lap and took the vital single point that went with it.

On his form that day Moss could have beaten Hawthorn's fastest lap but he misread the signalling board from the Vanwall pit 'HAWT-REC' (Hawthorn Record Lap). Moss read the board as 'HAW REG' (Hawthorn Regular) and made no effort to beat Hawthorn's time of 2 min. 32.37 sec., an average speed of 108.741 m.p.h., and only two-tenths of a second faster than Moss's best lap. The outcome of it all was that Moss scored eight points for a win but Hawthorn was only one point behind—with 7 points for second place and fastest lap.

Hawthorn was very nearly disqualified at Oporto and he would then have lost his 7 points and Moss would have led the World Championship but Moss—great sportsman that he is—gave evidence in favour of Hawthorn.

On his last lap Hawthorn spun, then stalled, and was accused of restarting in the opposite direction of the race. However, Moss saw what happened and emphatically stated that his rival had not broken the rules because he was not on the actual circuit when he restarted. A grateful and relieved Hawthorn kept his 7 points.

The total of points over the season was now Hawthorn 37, Moss 32. We shall see later on why that point for fastest lap was so important.

The next championship race was the Italian Grand Prix at Monza and it was there that Tony Brooks won again, averaging 121.215 m.p.h. in his Vanwall for just over two hours. In the opening stages Moss and Hawthorn fought a tremendous duel for the lead until on lap 17 of the seventy lap race Moss pulled into the pits with gearbox trouble and retired.

It was Brooks who saved the day for Vanwall and kept the championship still open for Moss. For if Hawthorn had won, then the World Championship would have been his with an unassailable total of points. The outcome of the next and final race of the season—at Casablanca—would not have mattered. So Brooks turned on the heat and went after the Ferrari, his Vanwall the only one still in the race for Lewis-Evans was out as well as Moss.

From fifth place Brooks edged his way forward lap by lap, and when Hawthorn made a pit stop of forty-five seconds for tyres, Brooks was well in the picture. On lap 40, with thirty still to go, he was lying third and only ten seconds behind Hawthorn, with Masten Gregory's Maserati between the Ferrari and Vanwall. On lap 46 the Vanwall was second—spectator Moss in the pits suddenly aware that the tremendous effort Brooks was making might well snatch victory from Hawthorn.

With ten laps to go, Brooks and Hawthorn were neck and neck at the pits. Then Brooks was out in front, and Hawthorn -with a slipping clutch—could not hold him. Brooks took the chequered flag and 8 points whilst Hawthorn in second place had to be content with 6. Early in the race the American Phil Hill, driving a Ferrari, had clocked a fantastic 125 m.p.h. lap, and Hawthorn's slipping clutch had prevented him from bettering Hill's time and winning the point for fastest lap.

And so, with nine races run, the World Championship would be decided at Casablanca the following month on the Ain-Diab circuit. This gave motor-racing journalists and enthusiasts all over the world plenty of time to work out what might happen, for the 1958 points system, which determined the winner, laid down that although a driver could gain points in each championship event throughout the season, his final total would be made up of points gained in his six best placings. And the Grand Prix of Morocco at Casablanca was the final event of the season.

The chart on the opposite page shows that Hawthorn had scored in eight events up to and including the Italian Grand Prix and that the points from his six best placings totalled 40. Even if Hawthorn failed to score any points at Casablanca his total would remain unchanged.

Moss had scored 32 points—but in only five events—so that points gained at Casablanca could be added to his total of best placings. In the unlikely event of Hawthorn not scoring any points, Moss knew that he would have to win, and put up fastest lap as well, so that he could add 9 points to his total of 32 for his six best placings—making 41 points, just one better than Hawthorn. If Moss did not get that one vital point for fastest lap, then he could not win the championship. For to win the race without fastest lap would only enable him to reach a total of 40 points and thus tie with

Hawthorn. In this eventuality the championship would have gone to Hawthorn for he had scored in more races during the 1958 season than Moss.

So Moss knew exactly what he had to do; score the maximum possible number of 9 points by winning and getting fastest lap. But what about Hawthorn? He was in the fortunate position of not having to win in order to clinch the championship. In fact, if he took six points for second place, the championship would be his even if Moss won the race and put up fastest lap.

THE WORLD CHAMPIONSHIP TABLE FOR 1958, AS IT STOOD BEFORE THE GRAND PRIX OF MOROCCO

	ARGENTINE	MONACO	DUTCH	BELGIAN	FRENCH	BRITISH	GERMAN	PORTUGUESE	ITALIAN	TOTAL POINTS	TOTAL OF SIX BEST PLACINGS
HAWTHORN	4(3rd)	1(F)	2(5th)	6(2nd) 1(F)	8(1st) 1(F)	6 (2nd) 1(F)		6(2nd) 1(F)	6(2nd)	43	40
MOSS	8(1st)		8(1st) 1(F)		6(2nd)		1(F)	8(1st)		32	32

POINT SCORING

8 points for 1st place
6 points for 2nd place
4 points for 3rd place
3 points for 4th place
2 points for 5th place

1 point for fastest lap (F)

The chart shows that the least valuable of Hawthorn's six best performances was in the Argentine where he scored only 4 points. All Hawthorn had to do was score 6 points for second place at Casablanca and he could then substitute these points for the 4 Argentine points, thus increasing his total of six best performances from 40 to 42. Moss could not equal this total under any circumstances.

The picture would have been a very different one if Moss had scored that one vital point at Oporto, thus increasing his total of six best performances to 33, and Hawthorn had lost it, thus reducing the total for his six best to 39. Of course, if Moss had not supported Hawthorn at Oporto when the Ferrari driver stalled and was accused of restarting in the opposite direction of the race, Hawthorn would have lost his seven points, leaving the championship wide open at Casablanca. After the Oporto race Hawthorn would have had 30 points and Moss 32. But such is motor-racing and such is the sportsmanship of men like Stirling Moss and Mike Hawthorn.

As the date of the race drew near the Moss-Hawthorn duel was given a great deal of publicity in the press for it had captured the public imagination. People who had never shown any interest in motor-racing were eagerly awaiting the race and trying to work out what Moss had to do and what Hawthorn had to do in order to clinch the championship.

At the Steering Wheel Club in London where drivers, patrons and enthusiasts gather between races, most people were agreed that Hawthorn deserved to win the championship. The 'Farnham Flyer' had put up a fine performance over the season, and a consistent one, scoring points in every championship race with the exception of that tragic German Grand Prix. No other driver contesting the championship had scored in so many races, and no other driver had been faced with such adversity. Musso killed at Rheims...Collins (Mon ami mate as Hawthorn called him) at the Nurburgring.

By carrying on after these two fatalities and, incidentally, holding together what remained of the sadly depleted and demoralised Ferrari *équipe,* Hawthorn ignored what can only be described as a truly frightening chain of events. It was not surprising when early in October the *élite* Guild of Motoring Writers voted Mike Hawthorn 'Driver of the Year'—a title held by Fangio in 1957.

By mid-October the Grand Prix 'circus' was on the way to Morocco and the very fast 4.7 mile Ain-Diab road circuit, six miles from the centre of Casablanca. Most of the drivers had raced at Ain-Diab the previous year when Asian 'flu prevented Moss from taking part and attacked Fangio, Hawthorn, Collins and Schell as well. Behra had won for Maserati at an average speed of 112.65 m.p.h. but it was not a world championship event.

On the Friday afternoon before the race, and under a blazing hot sun, the cars came out for the first practice session. The main interest was in the Vanwalls, Ferraris and B.R.M.s; Vanwalls for Moss, Brooks and Lewis-Evans; Ferraris for Hawthorn, Phil Hill and Gendebien; and B.R.M.s for Behra, Schell, Bonnier and Flockhart.

Behra, Moss and Hawthorn were soon out on the circuit and it was Behra who put up the fastest lap of the day—a very determined Behra who was going to do *his* best to win the race and was quite unconcerned about the whys and wherefores of the forthcoming battle between Moss and Hawthorn. His time of 2 min. 25.2 sec. was four-tenths of a second faster than Fangio's 1957 circuit record but there was quite a lot of scrapping before the others gave best to the tough little Frenchman.

Moss and Hawthorn set the pace at around 2 min. 32 sec., then Hawthorn chopped off two seconds. Brooks—motoring very confidently—got the time down to 2 min. 28.5 sec., then down again to 2 min. 26.7 sec. Brooks was really on form and knocked another second and a fraction off to equal Fangio's 1957 record lap of 2 min. 25.6 sec., a scorching average of 116.8 m.p.h. Hawthorn got down to 2 min. 25.7 sec., but Moss was not yet in the picture.

Towards the end of practice the fast boys all went out together—Brooks, Hawthorn, Behra, Moss, Schell and Phil Hill—and it was then that Behra showed them all the

The very fast Ain-Diab, [Ca]sablanca circuit on the Atlantic coast was the rather featureless setting for the last World [Ch]ampionship event of 1958, and a needle match between Moss [(Van]wall) and Hawthorn (Ferrari) for the Championship.

(Geoffrey Goddard)

Stuart Lewis-Evans clarifies a [po]int with a Vanwall mechanic. Sadly, Lewis-Evans crashed on [la]p 42 when his engine blew up and he was badly burned. He was flown to London but succumbed to his injuries.

(Geoffrey Goddard)

On the 18th lap, a third of the race distance, Moss (Vanwall) was in the lead by fourteen seconds from Phil Hill [(F]errari) when he collided with Seidel's Maserati, [bei]ng lapped for the second [t]ime. The Vanwall's nose [w]as crumpled and Moss [was] warned by his pit to 'WATCH TEMP', but fortunately no serious damage had been done.

(Geoffrey Goddard)

◀

*Enzo Ferrari was quick to spot
potential of Mike Hawthorn an
signed him for Ferrari in 1953
The 'Commendatore' was the
driving force behind the cars f
the Maranello factory that bore
insignia of the Prancing Horse*
(Geoffrey Goddard)

*The points system dictated race
strategy for Hawthorn in his bi
against Moss for the
Championship. Provided he
finished second—even if Moss
the race and fastest lap—the
Championship would be his.*
(Geoffrey Goddard)

▼

◀

*Moss takes the chequered flag fo
Vanwall, a resounding 1 minu
24 seconds ahead of Hawthorn
Ferrari. Moss took the lead from
the start and was never in dang
of losing it. He drove superbly,
the very top of his form, and eas
held off the Ferrari of Phil Hill
until the American was signalle
to fall back so that Hawthorn
could move in behind the
Vanwall. Now Moss led Hawtho
by 71 seconds and went on to u
the race—also fastest lap—whil
Hawthorn took the vital six poir
for second place and became
World Champion Driver for 195*
(Geoffrey Goddard)

quick way round. Practice ended with Moss making one final effort to beat Behra's time but only managing 2 min. 26 sec. The little Frenchman was 'tops' that day.

On Saturday the duel for pole position on the starting grid was renewed. Lewis-Evans went round in 2 min. 27 sec., then Moss went out and blew up his engine. No need to worry—Vanwall chopped and changed the cars so that Moss took over Brooks's car, Brooks took Lewis-Evans's car, and Lewis-Evans took the spare.

Moss, in the Brooks car, was soon down to 2 min. 25.7 sec., Hawthorn fighting back with 2 min. 25.3 sec. Then Behra and Bonnier both streaked round in their B.R.Ms in 2 min. 25 sec. exactly. This was almost as exciting as a full-length Grand Prix and when Moss went out again in the Vanwall, and clocked 2 min. 23.2 sec., and Brooks did 2 min. 24.9 sec., it was obvious that this Moroccan Grand Prix of 1958 was going to be a sizzler. Hawthorn topped them all with 2 min. 23.1 sec., a tenth of a second quicker than Moss's Vanwall. And when the practice session ended it was still Hawthorn with the fastest time of the day, and no less than eight drivers had bettered Fangio's 1957 record lap!

On Sunday, soon after two o'clock, the drivers were presented to the King of Morocco and already a vast crowd of 100,000 had settled down in the grandstands and enclosures around the circuit. Arabs in their long flowing 'nighshirt' robes gathered in small groups at vantage points, lending an air of unreality to this twentieth-century battle between men and machines.

As the cars lined up on the grid—Hawthorn, Moss and Lewis-Evans on the front row, Behra and Phil Hill on the second row, and Gendebien, Brooks and Bonnier on the third—King Mohammed sat in the royal box, surrounded by his entourage and protected by his personal bodyguard. It was a colourful spectacle.

At 2.50 the flag dropped and Lewis-Evans shot into the lead, Moss almost level with him—a grim determined Moss who must have felt a great wave of relief now that at last the race was on. For surely few drivers have ever been under such a strain during the weeks and days prior to a race, knowing that the only hope of winning lay in victory *and* fastest lap. Now the waiting was over and Stirling Moss proceeded to drive one of the finest races of his life.

As the pack went into the first corner, a right-hand one, Moss led Phil Hill—the American having streaked through from the second row of the grid at the start; and as the field streamed uphill and then down again along the Boulevard Panoramique it was still Moss, then Hill. Right again on to the Azemmour-Casablanca main road, Hill closing the gap foot by foot, Moss calm, collected.

As the Vanwall and Ferrari turned right again and streaked towards the Sidi Abderhaman curve and the coast road, Hill was very close. And at the end of that tremendous first lap as Moss streaked along the coast road, the blue Atlantic on his left,

Hill closed right up and the Vanwall and Ferrari passed the pits side by side. Almost immediately the rest of the fast boys streamed by—Hawthorn's Ferrari, Bonnier's B.R.M., the Vanwalls of Brooks and Lewis-Evans, then Behra's B.R.M.

The seconds ticked by and then the green Vanwall came into view again, Moss holding off Hill's challenge, Hill driving on the limit. Just after the two cars had scorched by the pits at the end of their second lap, Hill left his braking too late at Ain-Diab Corner and shot up the escape road. During the four seconds that it took Hill to get back on to the circuit, Hawthorn and Bonnier tore past. In the lead still, Moss pulled out all the stops, thankful that Hill was no longer riding his tail but well aware that Hawthorn was only a second or two behind.

Relentlessly Moss opened out the gap between his Vanwall and Hawthorn's Ferrari whilst Hill fairly burned up the road in his efforts to get back into second place so as to harass Moss again. For this was the Ferrari strategy: Hill to worry Moss and get that vital fastest lap—Hawthorn to stay back until it was time for him to take second place and with it the World Championship.

With eight laps completed, and the race average not far short of 116 m.p.h., Hill had passed Bonnier and Hawthorn and was in second place again. Not that this worried Moss unduly for he was way out in front, handling the speeding Vanwall in that calm, detached way of his that is the hallmark of a really great driver. And, not very far behind, Tony Brooks was moving up in his Vanwall with the task of wedging himself in second place and staying there at all costs.

This, then, was the race pattern. Moss and Brooks versus Hawthorn and Hill; Vanwall versus Ferrari; the prize—the World Championship of Drivers.

Ten laps completed and Moss led Hill by nine seconds at an average of 116.25 m.p.h. Five laps later and he was ten seconds out in front, having set up a new lap record of 2 min. 24 sec., which Hill then bettered with 2 min. 23.3 sec. Meanwhile, Brooks had passed Bonnier's B.R.M.—no easy task for Bonnier was driving a fine race on the very top of his form. Now Brooks had Hawthorn in his sights and slowly but surely he began to close on the tail of the Ferrari.

On lap 17 Brooks drew alongside the Ferrari and took Hawthorn for third place. Now for Hill's Ferrari. Out in front Moss was involved in an incident that could have cost him the race. As he lapped Seidel's Maserati the two cars collided, and whilst Seidel crawled round to his pit the Vanwall went on its way with a crumpled nose. Out went the signal board from the Vanwall pit 'Watch Temp' (watch the temperature gauge in case the collision causes overheating). But fortunately no serious damage had been done.

Moss continued his meteoric progress, setting up a new lap record of 2 min. 22.9 sec. on lap 20 of this fifty-three-lap race. By now the race had been under way for forty-eight minutes and Moss led Hill by 13.4 seconds at an average of 117.1 m.p.h., whilst the Ferrari led Brooks's Vanwall by eighteen seconds. Brooks had got to start closing the gap pretty smartly if he wanted to get out front with Moss who shattered the lap record again on lap 21 and left it at 2 min. 22.5 sec., a tremendous 119.334 m.p.h.

Just before half distance, with twenty-five laps completed, Moss had increased his lead over Hill to twenty seconds, but Brooks had been unable to close on Hill and was in dire trouble with Hawthorn. As much as he wanted to avoid a fierce duel with Brooks that might force the Ferrari out of the race, Hawthorn had got to dislodge the Vanwall from its key position between the two Ferraris and on lap 26 Hawthorn passed Brooks into third place. Now Moss had two Ferraris on his tail again.

Two laps later the Vanwall was right on the Ferrari's tail, Brooks very much aware that half the race was run and that he had precious little time in which to displace Hawthorn and then deal with Hill's Ferrari. For another two laps—five shattering minutes—Hawthorn and Brooks fought tooth and nail for third place, a duel that was in fact the turning point of the race. For on lap 30 the Vanwall went past the pits with puffs of black smoke coming from the exhaust. Shortly afterwards the Vanwall engine—stressed beyond the limit—blew up with a bang and Brooks found himself controlling a monumental slide as the engine spewed oil on to the road.

Brooks held the car superbly and stopped on the edge of the road, bitterly disappointed in himself (but unjustly so) for not having dealt with Hawthorn, thus pushing back the Ferrari to fourth place. No one could have tried harder to help his team leader than Brooks did that afternoon.

With Brooks out of the running, Hawthorn sat securely in third place whilst Hill kept second place warm for him, nearly half a minute behind Moss. It was virtually all over bar the shouting—and poor Moss must have known it—for unless Hawthorn blew up or ran off the road, which was most unlikely, then very shortly the Ferrari pit would slow down Hill so that Hawthorn could move up into second place.

There were two outside chances that could save Moss—but neither was very likely. Bonnier, still driving a great race, was lying fourth and might possibly be able to catch for third place—thus taking over where Brooks had left off. But neither B.R.M. nor Bonnier were likely to mix it with Hawthorn's Ferrari in order to secure the championship for Moss—particularly if it jeopardised the fourth place which Bonnier had earned so well.

The other outside chance was Lewis-Evans, the third Vanwall driver, in fifth place behind Bonnier. But Lewis-Evans would have to do some very fast motoring indeed to catch Bonnier—let alone Hawthorn. At this stage of the race only Moss, Hill, Hawthorn, Bonnier and Lewis-Evans were on the same lap. The terrific average put up by the leading cars had outstripped the rest of the field, leaving some drivers five laps in arrears and one eight laps behind.

The Ferrari team manager now played his trump card, for it was quite clear that Hill was not going to catch Moss or force him to blow up. A signal went out to Hill, ordering him to slow down so that Hawthorn could catch up and take that vital second place. And so we had the picture of Moss out in front, still going like the wind, and Hill dropping back to let Hawthorn through. It took four laps to complete the manoeuvre, for Hill had forced a large gap between his Ferrari and Hawthorn, but when it was completed there was Mike Hawthorn sitting in second place with the World Championship practically in his lap.

At forty laps the race order was Moss, Hawthorn, Hill, Bonnier and Lewis-Evans in the first five places, with Moss two miles ahead of Hawthorn. Then, with only twenty-five minutes of racing still to go, Lewis-Evans crashed on the back leg of the circuit. Black smoke belched skywards as the rescue helicopter took off, for already the Vanwall was blazing fiercely and poor Lewis-Evans had been terribly burned. He was rushed to hospital, then flown back to London in Tony Vandervell's chartered Viscount. Within seven days he had succumbed to his injuries.

With Lewis-Evans out of the race, Moss continued on his victorious way with the remaining Vanwall, slowing his lap times by six or seven seconds in the closing laps so that he was circulating in a comfortable 2 min. 30 sec., but still some three miles—almost a lap—ahead of Hawthorn. When Moss took the chequered flag and led Hawthorn over the line by 1 min. 24.7 sec. he knew he could have done no more, for he had never once lost the lead in 250 miles of flat-out racing and had taken fastest lap as well—but he had lost the championship by a single point. The final score was Hawthorn 42 points, Moss 41 points. It was some consolation to Moss that his victory clinched the Manufacturer's Cup for Vanwall.

When Hawthorn crossed the line, with Hill's Ferrari less than a second behind, he gave himself—the first British driver to win the World Championship—a boxer's salute. It had been an exhilarating day but a day full of drama and clouded by the accident to Lewis-Evans. If the truth were known, Moss and Hawthorn were probably very, very glad that it was all over.

Three months after becoming World Champion—and having just retired from the sport of motor-racing—Mike Hawthorn died in a road accident, and many thousands of enthusiasts mourned the loss of one of the greatest and most colourful drivers in the history of the sport.

Results
53 Laps

1.	S. MOSS	VANWALL	2 HR 09 MIN 15.1 SEC
			187.427 KPH (116.461 MPH)
2.	J. M. HAWTHORN	FERRARI	2 HR 10 MIN 39.8 SEC
3.	P. HILL	FERRARI	2 HR 10 MIN 40.6 SEC
4.	J. BONNIER	B.R.M.	2 HR 11 MIN 01.8 SEC
5.	H. SCHELL	B.R.M.	2 HR 11 MIN 48.8 SEC
6.	M. GREGORY	MASERATI	52 LAPS
7.	R. SALVADORI	COOPER-CLIMAX	51 LAPS
8.	J. FAIRMAN	COOPER-CLIMAX	50 LAPS
9.	H. HERRMANN	MASERATI	50 LAPS
10.	C. ALLISON	LOTUS-CLIMAX	49 LAPS
11.	G. GERINI	MASERATI	48 LAPS
12.	G. HILL	LOTUS-CLIMAX	46 LAPS

FASTEST LAP: S. MOSS (VANWALL) ON LAP 21

2 MIN 22.5 SEC AT 192.050 KPH (119.334 MPH)

Retirements

M. TRINTIGNANT	COOPER-CLIMAX	LAP 10 - Engine
W. SEIDEL	MASERATI	LAP 16 - Collision with Moss
R. FLOCKHART	B.R.M.	LAP 16 - Engine
J. BEHRA	B.R.M.	LAP 27 -
C. A. S. BROOKS	VANWALL	LAP 30 - Engine
O. GENDEBIEN	FERRARI	LAP 30 - Engine
S. LEWIS-EVANS	VANWALL	LAP 42 - Engine blew up

Formula 2 Results

1.	J. BRABHAM	COOPER-CLIMAX	49 LAPS
2.	B. McLAREN	COOPER-CLIMAX	48 LAPS
3.	R. LACAZE	COOPER-CLIMAX	48 LAPS
4.	A. GUELFI	COOPER-CLIMAX	48 LAPS

Retirements

T. BRIDGER	COOPER-CLIMAX	LAP 29 - Multiple crash
F. PICARD	COOPER-CLIMAX	LAP 29 - Multiple crash

Chapter 12

MONACO GRAND PRIX
10 MAY 1959

The Circuit

MONTE CARLO

100 Laps of 3.138 KM

313.800 KM = 194.985 MILES

Over the years few motor-racing circuits in Europe have remained unchanged, with the exception of Monaco where the Grand Prix was run for the first time in 1929 and won by W. Williams (Bugatti) at an average speed of 49.83 mph. Even if the organisers wanted to make a major change, the tight-packed buildings and narrow streets of the Principality make it impossible.

In 1959 the race was won by Jack Brabham at an average speed of 66.711 mph and he put up fastest lap as well at 70.072 mph. This unique round-the-houses circuit which twists and turns through the narrow, winding streets of Monte Carlo is not only spectacular but colourful as well, with much of the circuit following the promenade and the quayside. The yachts offshore and in the harbour provide a splendid vantage point, and in the town every balcony is packed with spectators.

The start of a Monaco Grand Prix is an awe inspiring sight as sixteen cars—in a closely packed bunch, and jostling for position—rush along the short stretch of seafront towards the hairpin which takes them climbing up into the town.

The short, 1.9 mile circuit is an unforgiving one that leaves no margin for error. Walls, kerbs and houses impose a strict, unyielding limitation on race strategy, and passing places in the narrow streets are few and far between. It is not surprising that the grid at Monaco is limited to the fastest sixteen cars in practice.

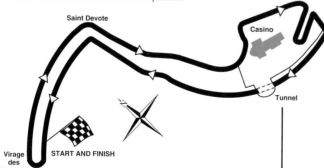

Starting Grid

J. BRABHAM COOPER-CLIMAX **1.40.1**	**J. BEHRA** FERRARI **1.40.0**	**S. MOSS** COOPER-CLIMAX **1.39.6**

P. HILL FERRARI **1.41.3**	**C. A. S. BROOKS** FERRARI **1.41.0**

R. SALVADORI COOPER-MASERATI **1.42.4**	**J. BONNIER** B.R.M. **1.42.3**	**M. TRINTIGNANT** COOPER-CLIMAX **1.41.7**

R. FLOCKHART B.R.M. **1.43.1**	**H. SCHELL** B.R.M. **1.43.0**

B. McLAREN COOPER-CLIMAX **1.43.9**	**W. VON TRIPS** PORSCHE FORMULA 2 **1.43.8**	**M. GREGORY** COOPER-CLIMAX **1.43.2**

C. ALLISON FERRARI FORMULA 2 **1.44.4**	**G. HILL** LOTUS-CLIMAX **1.43.9**

B. HALFORD
LOTUS-CLIMAX
FORMULA 2
1.44.8

NON - QUALIFIERS

I. BUEB COOPER-CLIMAX FORMULA 2 **1.44.9**	**G. SCARLATTI** MASERATI **1.45.0**
L. BIANCHI COOPER-CLIMAX FORMULA 2 **1.45.4**	**A. DE CHANGY** COOPER-CLIMAX FORMULA 2 **1.45.4**
MISS M. DE FILIPPIS PORSCHE R.S.K. FORMULA 2 **1.47.8**	**P. LOVELY** LOTUS-CLIMAX **1.47.9**
J. LUCIENBONNET COOPER-CLIMAX FORMULA 2 **1.50.9**	**A. TESTUT** MASERATI **1.59.1**

The Race of a Thousand Corners

*I*t is known as 'The Race of a Thousand Corners' and is one of the most spectacular and colourful world championship events of the season. Officially designated 'The Grand Prix of Monaco', this unique 'round-the-houses' race—run over a hundred laps of a narrow, winding 1.9-mile circuit in the centre of the Principality—is recognised as one of the toughest tests of car and driver in the world. For there are ten acute corners to every lap—a thousand corners in all—and the cars take terrific punishment as brakes, suspension, steering and gearbox are strained to the limit. The drivers dare not relax, for every lap of just under two miles demands anything from fifteen to twenty-two gear changes depending on the car and its gear ratios. It is not unusual for a driver to change gear 1,800 times during the course of a Monaco Grand Prix.

The tortuous circuit, bounded for most of its length by pavements, walls, kerbs, houses and balustrades, allows absolutely no margin for error. Within seconds of the flag dropping, the field is jockeying for position at the Gasworks Hairpin, then doubling back past the pits to Sainte Devote corner and Casino Bend—with the Hotel de Paris on the left and the famous Casino on the other side of the road. Then down past the Metropole, round the Station Hairpin and on to the Promenade. This is the fastest section of the course, and after running on to the quayside from the Promenade there is a tunnel where the maximum speed reached is in the region of 140 m.p.h.

Almost before the drivers have had time to accustom themselves again to the bright sunlight they have to brake for the chicane, an artificial obstacle on the quayside designed to slow them down. A left-turn as the circuit follows the quayside brings the cars back to the starting area and the Gasworks Hairpin.

All this in little more than a hundred seconds and anything up to twenty-two gear changes—an average of one every five seconds. No wonder the drivers reckon they

Brabham

work overtime at Monaco. Without a doubt they give good value for money, for the size and shape of the circuit is such that spectators who occupy the numerous vantage points on the balconies of hotels, *pensions* and private house—as well as those in the grandstands and enclosures—seldom have time to be bored. In this race there is something happening all the time.

The Monaco Grand Prix, young in years by Grand Prix standards, was run for the first time in 1929 and won by W. Williams (Bugatti) at an average speed of 49.83 m.p.h. for 198 miles. And in the comparatively few years that there has been motor-racing in the streets of Monte Carlo the unforgiving circuit has exacted a heavy toll. On two occasions—in 1936 and 1950—there have been multiple crashes involving up to half the entry, and in 1957 there was a triple crash at the chicane that put Hawthorn, Collins and Moss out of the race on the fourth lap.

The practice sessions for the 1957 race were by no means quiet, orderly affairs. On the first day of practice Moss rammed the chicane and damaged the training Vanwall; next day Jack Brabham of Australia went into the corner near the Casino too fast for the brakes and wrote off Rob Walker's brand-new, privately entered Formula 1 Cooper. Brabham was unhurt, as was Peter Collins when he lost control of his Lancia-Ferrari at the chicane. Fortunately a bollard halted the Italian car as it was about to topple into the harbour and Collins missed an almost certain ducking.

Two years earlier, in the 1955 race, Alberto Ascari had not been so fortunate. Eighty laps of the hundred-lap race had been run and Ascari was desperately trying to avoid being lapped by Stirling Moss in a Mercedes. The Italian, driving a Lancia, came out of the tunnel and swept down into the chicane too fast, suddenly swerved sideways into the hay bales, bounced off a stone bollard and toppled into the water, narrowly missing an anchored yacht.

The Lancia, with Ascari still in the cockpit, disappeared in a cloud of spray and steam. Fortunately, frogmen had been stationed at this point to deal with just such an eventuality, and as the blue helmet of Ascari bobbed above the water the frogmen rowed their boat towards him. The Italian struck out strongly and was soon safely in the boat—dazed and with an injured nose. After his miraculous escape it was a tragedy indeed when, a few days afterwards at Monza, Ascari crashed whilst practising in a Ferrari sports car and was killed.

Following the alarms and excursions during practice for the 1957 race, a field of sixteen cars lined up on the starting grid. Fangio's Maserati was in pole position, next to Collins (Lancia-Ferrari) and Moss (Vanwall); Hawthorn (Lancia-Ferrari) and Brooks (Vanwall) were on the second row. When the flag fell, the tightly packed bunch of cars surged into the hairpin and it was Moss who came out first, Fangio on his tail.

One...two...three laps—Moss out in front and going like the wind—and then high drama. Fangio came round in the lead, with Brooks behind him, but there was no sign of Moss, Hawthorn or Collins and there had indeed been a monumental pile-up. Streaking out of the tunnel in the lead, Moss braked for the chicane and suddenly realised that his brakes had locked. He hit the chicane with such force that poles and barricades shot into the air as though a land-mine had been exploded.

Collins, hard on the heels of Moss, just avoided the Vanwall but collected a flying piece of wood and rammed the barrier at the harbour's edge at the exact spot where he had crashed in practice. As a pole from the demolished barricade fell across the track, Brooks and Hawthorn arrived on the scene. Brooks slammed on the brakes of his Vanwall, but Hawthorn—taken by surprise—was unable to stop. A front wheel of the Lancia-Ferrari was torn off when it caught the back of the Vanwall, and as the wheel bounced into the harbour—just missing a startled official—Hawthorn's car crashed on top of Collins's Lancia-Ferrari on the very edge of the quayside.

As Brooks slowly accelerated away from the scene the wily Fangio picked his way carefully through the débris and settled down in the lead. And there he stayed whilst Brooks held second place and put up the best performance by a British driver in a British car in a world championship event for years. Vanwall were, in fact, only a few months away from their first victory in a championship event, the British Grand Prix of 1957 at Aintree, and the performance of Brooks at Monaco that Sunday was a real tonic to British motor-racing enthusiasts and a pointer to the Vanwall's brilliant future.

The triple crash and the magnificent driving of Brooks were not the only dramatic touches about the Monaco Grand Prix of 1957. Equally dramatic was the way in which Jack Brabham 'arrived' that day on the world championship scene.

After the new Formula 1 Cooper had been written-off on the Friday, Rob Walker's mechanic, Alf Francis, worked all through the night, transferring the 2-litre engine from the wrecked chassis to another car. And it was with this car that Brabham worked his way through to sixth place after only ten laps.

Admittedly the crash at the chicane had disposed of Moss, Hawthorn and Collins but, even so, Brabham's effort was most commendable. For he was showing a clean pair of heels to Gregory's $2\frac{1}{2}$-litre Maserati and Trintignant's $2\frac{1}{2}$-litre Lancia-Ferrari.

The crowd loved the way in which this impudent little Cooper, driven by an Australian, mixed it with the big boys. They cheered Brabham when he passed Flockhart's B.R.M., and after thirty laps the Cooper lay fourth. It really was incredible how the flying Cooper was so well up in the field after a third of the Monaco race against the cream of the world's Grand Prix drivers and cars. And so it went on. For another thirty-two laps a highly delighted Brabham tore round the Monaco circuit, and on lap 62 the Cooper was refuelled. Then he was away again, still going like a dingbat, but on lap 100 the Cooper packed up near the railway station when Jack Brabham was lying third.

What wretched luck—but Brabham was undismayed. He got out of the cockpit and started pushing, no mean task after three hours of really hard work on that tough

Monaco circuit. But the Australian was determined to finish—and finish he did—pushing the Cooper over the line in sixth place, shortly after Trintignant had passed him and taken fifth place.

We saw a little that day of the Brabham determination and guts that was to become part and parcel of the Grand Prix scene. The Australian was absolutely exhausted as he pushed the Cooper the last few yards to the line, and the crowd clapped and cheered his fine effort. Alf Francis found afterwards that the mounting of the fuel pump had been unable to stand the fatigue and had broken. Nevertheless, the little Cooper was one of only six of sixteen cars to finish. It had been a great performance.

The gay night life of Monte Carlo kept a lot of people up until the early hours of the morning. In the night clubs and bars, where the 'motor-racing crowd' always gather after a big race, the talk was of the way in which Fangio had sat back until the fierceness of the duel between Moss, Hawthorn and Collins had exploded in the wreckage of the Chicane, and of how Jack Brabham had almost snatched third place in his first world championship event. It was possible to pick up odd snatches of conversation; 'Quite a driver. Bit untidy but never mind...That Australian certainly makes Rob Walker's Cooper go like a bomb... Used to be a speedway ace or something... Very serious about it all... Hasn't got Moss's style'.

There were very few people in Monaco that night who knew anything about Jack Brabham for he is not one to talk about what he has done or what he intends to do. Brabham just gets on with the job and does it remarkably well.

He was born in Hurstville, a Sydney suburb, in April 1926, first drove a car at the age of twelve, was later apprenticed as a mechanic in a garage and then served with the Royal Australian Air Force as a flight mechanic in the war.

After the war Brabham met Johnnie Schonberg, an American midget-car speedway ace, and with Schonberg he visited a meeting in Brisbane. Very soon Jack Brabham was the youngest speedway ace on midget cars in Australia. For six years, until 1952, Brabham collected trophies in midget-car racing with almost monotonous regularity. Then he quit the speedways for circuit racing and built his own 'special', based on a Cooper. With this car he clinched the Redex Championship for winning more races in the 1952 season than any other driver, and encouraged by his success purchased a Cooper-Bristol, similar to the one in which Mike Hawthorn made *his* name in 1952 before joining Ferrari.

In 1953 and 1954 Brabham had a tremendous run of successes with the Cooper-Bristol, and in 1955 he arrived in Europe. I well remember the quiet Australian when he first raced over here, for his cornering technique was quite extraordinary. He hunched himself down in the cockpit as he had done in the days of midget car racing to avoid the sand and dirt thrown up by the rear wheels of cars in front.

Brabham returned to Australia at the end of 1955 to win the Australian Grand Prix but in 1956 he was back again in England. As a brilliant engineer, who had always tuned and maintained his own cars, Brabham joined the Cooper Car Company. He drove a 'works' sports car in certain races and in return worked on the team cars. Jack Brabham was IN; and although Charles and John Cooper did not know it, this was the beginning of a highly successful driver/constructor partnership that was to give Cooper cars the Formula 1 Championship, and Jack Brabham the title of World Champion, in 1959 and 1960. This then was the quiet young man who was discussed at such length by motor-racing enthusiasts after his plucky performance that Sunday afternoon. Few if any of them would have backed Brabham to win the World Championship within three years.

Brabham raced again at Monaco in 1958, this time in one of John Cooper's 'works' cars, but although he was fast enough to get the 2.2-litre Cooper-Climax on to the front row of the starting grid alongside Brooks (Vanwall) and Behra (B.R.M.) he was unlucky in the race. An anti-roll bar came adrift and the ensuing pit stop dropped the Australian out of the picture.

The race was a triumph for the Cooper-Climax entered by Rob Walker and driven by Trintignant. With Behra, Brooks, Moss and Hawthorn out of the race by half distance the plucky little Frenchman held the Ferraris of Musso and Collins at bay, never allowing them to get close enough to become a danger—driving the race of his life. It was perhaps the Frenchman's finest hour and the crowd went wild with excitement.

Once again the Monaco Grand Prix had taken its usual heavy toll of cars. All three Vanwalls failed to finish; Moss had engine trouble, the engine of the Lewis-Evans car was overheating, and Brooks was disqualified for endeavouring to start his car against the direction of the race after stopping out on the circuit with plug lead trouble. Behra's B.R.M. had brake trouble, Bonnier ran up on to the pavement with his Maserati and burst both front tyres, Scarlatti blew up the engine of his Maserati, Graham Hill's Lotus spun when the engine seized solid, Salvadori's gearbox failed on his 'works' Cooper, Hawthorn's Ferrari went out with a defective petrol pump, and the engine of the Von Trips Ferrari seized solid just before the finish.

Once again Jack Brabham's Cooper was one of only six of sixteen cars to finish, but this time he was fourth, three laps behind Trintignant, Musso and Collins.

In 1959, on his third appearance at Monaco, Brabham was on the threshold of a highly successful season. In fact the man from 'down under' was now ready to make his challenge for championship honours. The Monaco Grand Prix on May 10 opened the World Championship season, for there was no Argentine Grand Prix in 1959, and the British *équipes* journeyed to the little Principality with high hopes of a victory to launch the 1959 season on a firm footing. For 1958 had been Britain's Golden Year, with Mike Hawthorn the first Englishman to win the title of World Champion, whilst the

Manufacturers Cup—for the best performance over the season—had gone to Vanwall.

Like Mercedes-Benz at the end of 1955 and Maserati at the end of 1957, Vanwall had pulled out of motor-racing at the height of their success. Only Cooper, B.R.M. and Lotus remained to challenge Enzo Ferrari's cars, but only a week before Monaco, at Silverstone in the International Trophy, the $2\frac{1}{2}$-litre Cooper-Climax driven by Jack Brabham had soundly beaten the Ferraris.

This was the picture when the first practice session was held under a cloudy sky on the Thursday afternoon. As always at Monaco the field for such a dangerously narrow and winding circuit is limited to the fastest sixteen cars in practice, and this means that drivers have to try very hard right up to the last minute—particularly those at the slow end for they are liable to lose their place on the grid during the last minutes of the third and final session.

For a few laps it was comparatively peaceful—with most of the drivers getting the feel once again of this very 'dicey' circuit—and then the fireworks started. Schell, in a B.R.M., got down to 1 min. 47 sec.—some six seconds slower than the predicted best practice time based on the fastest lap of 1 min, 40.6 sec. in the 1958 race. Moss, with the Rob Walker Cooper-Climax, and Behra (Ferrari) soon made a nonsense of this time, Moss getting down to 1 min. 41.7 sec. and Behra immediately chopping off another tenth of a second.

Moss was not slow to accept the challenge and out he went again, hurling the Cooper round the 1.9-mile circuit in a most alarming fashion and finally getting his time down to 1 min. 41.1 sec. Meanwhile there had been a heart-stopping incident in the tunnel when Tony Brooks pulled over in his Ferrari to pass a slower car and spun in the darkness on some loose gravel. Brooks held the Ferrari and came out of the tunnel nose first but considerably shaken. Even so he managed second fastest time of the day and, when practice ended, the best laps had been clocked by Moss, Brooks and Behra.

On Friday Brabham decided that it was time he did some rapid motoring and streaked round the circuit, looking very much at home, in 1 min. 40.9 sec. This was quite a sizzler but not Brabham's best by any means; before the end of practice he had done even better with a time of 1 min. 40.1 sec. The Australian made it all look so easy and seemed to have no difficulty in keeping the Ferraris of Phil Hill, Tony Brooks and Behra out of the picture, or the B.R.M.s of Bonnier and Schell.

Stirling Moss had no intention of letting Brabham get pole position on the grid, and on Saturday—in the third and final practice session—Moss took the Cooper round in 1 min. 39.6 sec., thus beating Brabham's time. Not to be outdone, Behra also put everything he knew into one blistering lap and got down to 1 min. 40 sec. Towards the end of practice everyone seemed to be on the circuit—the faster drivers trying to beat Moss's time for pole position and the slower drivers trying to beat each other for the sixteenth place on the grid.

The Race of a Thousand Corners

TOP RIGHT

...ra (Ferrari) leads the Coopers of
...Moss and Brabham through the
...ists and turns at the Hotel Mira-
...eau. The Coopers were never far
...bind Bebra, and on lap 21 Moss
...k him approaching the chicane.
...Four laps later Bebra retired.

(LAT Photographic) ▶

...At three quarter distance Moss
...Cooper-Climax) was one minute
...ahead of Brabham, with Brooks
...(Ferrari) third. Soon after, Moss
...s out of the race. With Brabham
...only ten seconds ahead, Brooks
...led out all the stops in spite of
...eing almost overcome by beat
...and fumes in the cramped
...kpit of the Ferrari. But on this
...uit Brabham had the measure
...of Brooks and went on to win.

...r twenty-five laps Bebra held the
...Coopers of Moss and Brabham at
...bay, on a winding and narrow
...rcuit that was much more suited
...to the smaller cars.

(Geoffrey Goddard) ▼

▶

...bough Moss had pole position on
...be grid with his Cooper-Climax it
...as Bebra (Ferrari) who got away
...first, out-accelerating Moss and
...bham and surging into the lead.
...In the early stages, alongside the
...arbour, Bebra's Ferrari holds off
...ss whilst Brabham lies back and
...plays a waiting game.

(Geoffrey Goddard)

Dead car park at Les Princes. A
only two laps all three Formula
cars were involved in a multiple
pile up at Saint Devote. W. Von
Trips (Porsche) spun on an oil
patch, Cliff Allison in a Ferrari
avoiding action and hit the wall
and Bruce Halford rammed the
Ferrari with his Lotus-Climax. T
three badly damaged cars were
manhandled on to the pavemen
and their drivers—fortunately n
seriously hurt—became spectato
(LAT Photographic)

Although Brabham did not take
lead until Moss was out of the ro
the Australian was absolutely at
home on the Monaco circuit an
never put a wheel wrong. In
practice and during the race he
had no difficulty keeping the
Ferraris and B.R.Ms at bay, and
race day he put up fastest lap at
late stage when there was a lot a
oil and rubber on the track
(Geoffrey Goddard)

In the midst of all this win-or-bust racing, Brabham lost control of his Cooper as he braked for the Gasworks Hairpin. The car spun, then ran backwards—still spinning—into the straw bales. The imperturbable Australian kept the engine running and was soon back in the fray, but was unable to better his Friday time of 1 min. 40.1 sec. At any rate he was on the front row of the grid with Moss and Behra, and most of the knowledgeable enthusiasts reckoned that the winner of the International Trophy stood a good chance of winning the Monaco Grand Prix if he could get out in front at the start.

That night, after practice, Tony Brooks emphasised that the Monaco circuit was obviously more suited to the smaller, handier Coopers than to the Ferraris, and most people agreed with him. On that basis the battle looked like being between Moss and Brabham.

There is no more colourful setting for the start of a motor-race than Monte Carlo. Gay, lighthearted crowds pour into the Principality from early morning—by bus, train and private car from all parts of the Riviera—until the side streets running into the circuit are jammed full of parked cars. Scores of extra gendarmes control the crowds. Soon every vantage point is taken; windows, balconies, roof-tops—even the masts of yachts in the harbour. And all this against a backcloth of the Alps Maritime, multi-coloured houses clustered on the slopes around the circuit, the castle of Prince Rainier and Princess Grace, and the waters of the crowded harbour, shimmering in the sunlight, with the Mediterranean beyond.

In brilliant sunshine and under a bright blue sky the cars were wheeled out on to the grid whilst the loudspeakers blared dance music, and an enormous crowd—en fête and in high spirits—crammed the enclosure behind Gasworks Hairpin to bursting point. Prince Rainier and Princess Grace toured the circuit in their Rolls-Royce and then it was time for the seventeenth Grand Prix of Monaco.

It was a compact grid—only sixteen cars—and when the starter dropped his flag they surged into the Gasworks Hairpin in a tight, closely-packed bunch, only inches separating one car from another. It was Jean Behra who reached the hairpin first, the nose of his Ferrari fractionally ahead of Moss's Cooper. As Behra swung the wheel over to the right and accelerated, Moss was on his tail, then Brabham, and in this order they passed the Royal Box.

The cavalcade of thundering racing cars, still in a fairly tight bunch and likely to be for a lap or so, swept up through St. Devote to Casino Bend, then down past the Metropole Hotel and through the Station Hairpin to the Promenade.

Into the tunnel—Behra, Moss, Brabham—and out again with the velocity of cannon balls. Through the chicane and on to the quayside they swept—the red Ferrari still out in front—and soon they were passing the Royal Box again.

One lap completed, ninety-nine to go, and suddenly the field of sixteen was reduced by three cars. As Von Trips, in a Formula 2 Porsche, headed up the hill from St. Devote to the Casino for the second time, he suddenly felt the Porsche slewing helplessly sideways, right in front of Allison's Formula 2 Ferrari and Halford's Formula 2 Lotus. There was freshly dropped oil on the road!

Allison, a split second before he would have rammed the Porsche amidships, wrenched the steering wheel and hit the wall instead, and a split second later Halford ran into the Ferrari. All three drivers were lucky to escape without serious injury but the cars were completely wrecked, and what a blessing that they had been bringing up the tail end of the field.

And then there were thirteen.

Within a minute of the crash, whilst the three damaged cars were being manhandled on to the pavement, the leaders went by again. Behra was still in front, the Ferrari driver looking understandably harassed with Moss on his tail, whilst Brabham tore round behind Moss, looking absolutely at ease. By now the three leaders had pulled away from the rest of the field which was headed by Phil Hill's Ferrari and Trintignant's Cooper-Climax.

The hectic pace was beginning to tell and Masten Gregory was the next driver to retire. With only seven laps completed he coasted his Cooper into the pits without clutch or gearbox.

And then there were twelve.

Out in front the high-speed trio tore round the narrow circuit in close company and seldom more than a length separated each car. The crowd loved it, particularly as a Frenchman was out in the lead—even if he was driving an Italian car. In the pits the lap scorers marked off their charts—ten...fifteen...twenty laps—and still Behra, Moss and Brabham were secure in the first three places. Phil Hill in fourth place was half a minute behind Brabham, whilst Brooks's Ferrari was thirteen seconds behind Hill. Then came Schell's B.R.M., right on the Ferrari's tail.

Two laps later Moss slammed by Behra into the lead, and Brabham was not slow to follow suit. The Ferrari was in real trouble and as Behra started his twenty-fifth lap— with three-quarters of the race still to be run—the engine blew up and spewed oil on to the course at the Gasworks Hairpin.

And then there were eleven.

On the other side of the circuit, near the Station Hairpin, an oil pipe broke on Graham Hill's Lotus and the car burst into flames. Hill grabbed the extinguisher from the cockpit, put out the fire and walked back to the pits.

And then there were ten.

Now Moss displayed that faultless style of his that we have so often seen when the car is right and he is on top of his form. As dozens of journalists put a stop-watch on the gap between Moss and Brabham it soon became apparent that Moss intended to get way out in front, for he started widening the gap by two seconds a lap. With thirty laps completed, nearly a third of the race distance, Moss led Brabham by sixteen seconds, whilst the Australian led Phil Hill by twenty-six seconds, and Hill led Schell's B.R.M. and Brooks's Ferrari by just over half a minute. Even so, the race was only fifty-two minutes old and a lot could happen in the next two hours particularly if the Moss gremlin entered the fray.

On lap 37 Phil Hill lost his third place when he spun the Ferrari backwards into the straw bales at the right-angle turn just beyond the Hotel de Paris in the Casino Square. He was lucky for he had spun at the top of a hill leading down to the railway station; shouting at bystanders to keep their hands off the car (if they had helped him the penalty would have been disqualification) he got it rolling again, jumped into the cockpit and coaxed the engine into life. The American now had Schell and Brooks right on his dented tail and they soon passed him, duelling mightily for the third place he had vacated. A few laps later Hill, to the delight of the spectators, did it again at the same turn and once more he was able to push-start his Ferrari.

Harry Schell, with the B.R.M., was not so fortunate. On lap 46 Brooks slammed his Ferrari past the B.R.M. into third place and pulled away from Schell. This was not what the B.R.M. driver had planned and he pulled out all the stops, determined to dislodge the Ferrari and get a British car back into third place. He was unsuccessful for he hit the straw bales head on at the Casino and ripped off the nose piece of the B.R.M. This was not all; both the oil and water radiators had been split in the crash and the B.R.M.s race was run. Meanwhile, Bonnier's B.R.M. had retired at the pits with no brakes.

And then there were eight.

With fifty laps completed, half distance, Moss led Brabham by forty seconds; Brabham, in turn, led Brooks's Ferrari by thirty seconds. These were the only three cars on the same lap and it looked as though the race pattern was set for the remaining one and a half hours for Brabham did not appear anxious to try to catch Moss and was quite happily holding Brooks at bay.

The race was enlivened a little on lap 65 when Flockhart, in the last of the B.R.M.s, spun at the Casino, stalled the engine and was unable to restart the car by himself. He, like Bonnier, had also experienced brake trouble and had run off the course at the Gasworks Hairpin before spinning at the Casino. As Flockhart's B.R.M. was pushed off the course, one of the small group watching from the balcony of the Hotel de Paris was Juan Fangio, and one of the officials who pushed the car was Farina, the 1950 World Champion.

And then there were seven.

With eighty laps completed, the order was still Moss, Brabham and Brooks—no one else within two laps of them. At this stage of the race Brooks started to put on the pressure in a big way, determined to split the Cooper sandwich. Out came the stop-watches again for Brooks was only eleven seconds behind Brabham and there were still twenty laps to go. If anyone could do it, Brooks could.

Out in front, Moss also had twenty laps to go and then the Moss gremlin struck yet again and the Cooper pulled into the pits. Moss explained that there was a transmission vibration, but was sent off again to do another lap, still in the lead. Although there was nothing visibly wrong, Moss knew that his race was run. Within minutes he was back at his pit with the cryptic comment 'back axle', and the grinding noise from the rear end as the Cooper pulled in a second time was proof enough.

And then there were six.

Now Brabham came into his own, meeting and holding the challenge from Brooks, never putting a wheel wrong. There were eighteen laps to go and a gap to be closed of 10.5 seconds if Brooks wanted to wrest the lead from the Australian. Both the Ferrari and Cooper pits put out their 'faster' signal boards and Brabham immediately obliged with a tremendous lap of 1 min. 40.4 sec., an average speed of 70.072 m.p.h. and a new circuit record. At this stage of the race, with oil and rubber on the circuit, it was a remarkable time.

Brooks could do no more. The crowd knew nothing of the drama in the cockpit of the Ferrari where he was fighting a losing battle, not only against Brabham but against fumes as well. The heat and fumes in the enclosed cockpit of the Italian car, with its high sides, had been getting progressively worse during the race and, as the final laps ran out, Brooks was almost at the end of his tether.

He was physically sick—not once but several times—as Brabham reeled off the last few laps like a veteran and went on to win his first ever world championship event and nine points towards the 1959 Championship. Brooks gritted his teeth and stuck it out in the cockpit of the Ferrari, eventually crossing the line twenty seconds after Brabham but still on the same lap.

Once again, for the third time in succession, Brabham was one of the six finishers in Monaco's annual test of mechanical and physical endurance, but this time the man from 'down under' came home in first place after nearly three hours of hard racing.

It was the first victory of a 'works' Cooper from the Surbiton factory in a world championship event. The partnership of a car built by Charles and John Cooper, the superb Coventry-Climax engine, and Jack Brabham was in business. And what a partnership it turned out to be. By the end of the 1959 season Jack Brabham had clinched the coveted and prestigious World Championship, and the Cooper Car Company had been awarded the Manufacturer's Cup. And for good measure the *elite* Guild of Motoring Writers voted Jack Brabham 'Driver of the Year'.

Well might they say 'Jack's the boy'.

Results
100 Laps

1.	J. BRABHAM	COOPER-CLIMAX	2 HR 55 MIN 51.3 SEC
			107.361 KPH (66.711 MPH)
2.	C.A.S. BROOKS	FERRARI	2 HR 56 MIN 11.7 SEC
3.	M. TRINTIGNANT	COOPER-CLIMAX	98 LAPS
4.	P. HILL	FERRARI	97 LAPS
5.	B. Mc LAREN	COOPER-CLIMAX	96 LAPS
6.	R. SALVADORI	COOPER-MASERATI	83 LAPS

FASTEST LAP: J. BRABHAM (COOPER-CLIMAX) ON LAP 83
1 MIN 40.4 SEC AT 112.771 KPH (70.072 MPH)

Retirements

W. VON TRIPS	F.2 PORSCHE	LAP 2 - Multiple crash
C. ALLISON	F.2 FERRARI	LAP 2 - Multiple crash
B. HALFORD	F.2 LOTUS-CLIMAX	LAP 2 - Multiple crash
M. GREGORY	COOPER-CLIMAX	LAP 7 - Gearbox
G. HILL	LOTUS-CLIMAX	LAP 22 - Car on fire
J. BEHRA	FERRARI	LAP 25 - Engine
J. BONNIER	B.R.M.	LAP 46 - Brakes
H. SCHELL	B.R.M.	LAP 49 - Crashed
R. FLOCKHART	B.R.M.	LAP 65 - Spun - unable to restart
S. MOSS	COOPER-CLIMAX	LAP 82 - Rear axle

INDEX